Qualitative Analysis

Douglas Ezzy

Social Research Today edited by Martin Bulmer

The *Social Research Today* series provides concise and contemporary introductions to significant methodological topics in the social sciences. Covering both quantitative and qualitative methods, this new series features readable and accessible books from some of the leading names in the field and is aimed at students and professional researchers alike. This series also brings together for the first time the best titles from the old *Social Research Today* and *Contemporary Social Research* series edited by Martin Bulmer for UCL Press and Routledge.

Other series titles include:

Principles of Research Design in the Social Sciences Frank Bechhofer
 and Lindsay Paterson
Social Impact Assessment Henk Becker
The Turn to Biographical Methods in Social Science edited by Prue
 Chamberlayne, Joanna Bornat and Tom Wengraf
Quantity and Quality in Social Research Alan Bryman
Research Methods and Organisational Studies Alan Bryman
Field Research: A Sourcebook and Field Manual Robert G Burgess
In the Field: An Introduction to Field Research Robert G Burgess
Research Design second edition Catherine Hakim
Measuring Health and Medical Outcomes edited by Crispin Jenkinson
Methods of Criminological Research Victor Jupp
Information Technology for the Social Scientist edited by Raymond
 M Lee
An Introduction to the Philosophy of Social Research Tim May and
 Malcolm Williams
*Researching Social and Economic Change: The Uses of Household
Panel Studies* edited by David Rose
Surveys in Social Research fifth edition David de Vaus
Researching the Powerful in Education edited by Geoffrey Walford

Martin Bulmer is Professor of Sociology and co-director of the Institute of Social Research at the University of Surrey. He is also Academic Director of the Question Bank in the ESRC Centre for Applied Social Surveys, London.

Qualitative Analysis

Practice and innovation

Douglas Ezzy

First published 2002 by Routledge
11 New Fetter Lane, London EC4P 4EE
Simultaneously published in Australia and New Zealand by Allen & Unwin Ltd,
83 Alexander Street, PO Box 8500
Crows Nest, NSW 2065, Australia

Routledge is an imprint of the Taylor & Francis Group

© 2002 Douglas Ezzy

Typeset by Midland Typesetters, Victoria, Australia
Printed and bound by SRM Production Services, SDN, BHD, Malaysia

British Library Cataloguing in Publication Data
A catalogue record for this book is available from the British Library
ISBN 0-415-28126-1 (hbk)
ISBN 0-415-28127-X (pbk)

To Jill, who first taught me the value of listening to the 'other'.

Contents

List of figures

Introduction

'The Dance'

Her hands they trailed around the fire,
As she circled and spun webs of desire.
Transfixed I approached the forest clearing,
Observing carefully all I was seeing and hearing.

The fire burned bright on that cold clear night,
As she danced and chanted under the full moon light.
Noting moves, writing her words, with careful observation,
But all my distanced watching felt like voyeuristic deception.

She reached out her hand and drew my body and soul,
Into her circle and we became whole.
I feel the warmth of the fire, the earth under my feet,
As we dance and chant to the rhythm of her beat.

Next day I sit quietly at my desk to write,
Not about her, but with her, our encounter last night.
With passion and pleasure I recall our intimate romance,
Who can separate the observer, the dancer, and the dance?

(Doug Ezzy)

> The craft of a qualitative sociologist consists not of an objective methodology but of *hermeneutic practices* that permit the researcher to understand the indigenous world close to the way that it appears to the people themselves (Liberman 1999: 53, original emphasis).

> There is no choice between an 'engaged' and 'neutral' way of doing sociology. A non-committal sociology is an impossibility . . . Sociologists may deny or forget the 'world-view' effects of their work, and the impact of that view on human singular or joint actions, only at the expense of forfeiting that responsibility of choice which every other human being faces daily (Bauman 2000: 89).

Life fascinates me. How is it that we make our lives meaningful, finding dignity and purpose? How do we cope with the pain and anguish of loss, and how do we discover pleasure and joy? The sociological response to these questions is to point to relationships, shared culture, and social location. Life is found in relationships, real and imagined. Describing the social processes that make life meaningful is at the heart of good qualitative research.

The life of the qualitative researcher is no different from anyone else's life. Qualitative research is done through establishing relationships with people, places and performances. The best qualitative researchers do not separate their lives from their research, as if people could be understood through distancing ourselves from them. Qualitative research, and qualitative data analysis, involves working out how the things that people do make sense from their perspective. This can be done only by entering into their world, so that their world becomes our world. I do not mean that you have to become an unemployed person in order to research unemployed people, although it helps! Rather, that the interpretive process at the heart of qualitative data analysis involves trying to understand the practices and meanings of research participants from their perspective. Qualitative observation, and data analysis, is best done when the observer becomes part of the dance. Conducting qualitative research is about participating in other people's lives and writing about that participation.

I have used qualitative methods to study Pentecostal Christians, unemployed people, people living with HIV/AIDS, Witches and business practices. In each case I have attempted to understand how the people I have studied have made sense of their practices from their perspective. Now I have written a book about qualitative data analysis. I have tried to follow the same methodology in my study of qualitative methods. I have focused on how other qualitative researchers have made sense of their practices. That is to say, I have examined how other people have done qualitative data analysis—or at least what other researchers have written about what they have done.

This book engages in a dialogue between tradition and innovation. I demonstrate how the methods and theory of cultural studies, feminism, poststructuralism, postmodernism and hermeneutics can inform and enrich qualitative research methods. These innovative approaches are brought into dialogue with more established traditions such as ethnography, phenomenology, symbolic interactionism and grounded theory. This dialogue between tradition and innovation leads to a qualitative practice that is richer, more robust and more useful.

Discovery is a constant process of dialogue between the already known and the as yet unknown (this point is elaborated in detail in Chapter 1). I argue that one of the main challenges in qualitative data analysis is to ensure that the voice of the other is heard and allowed to enter into dialogue with preexisting understandings. It is seductively easy to discover what we, the researchers, expect to find. This seduction should be resisted. Rigorously conducted qualitative research listens attentively to 'the data' or to the 'other', and as a consequence reveals new understandings and builds new theory. It is also seductively easy to presume that 'new' discoveries have not been influenced by preexisting understandings. This seduction should also be resisted. Rigorously conducted qualitative research does not pretend to be uninfluenced by preexisting understandings. Rather, it actively engages these preexisting understandings, theories and assumptions, allowing them to be transformed and changed so that new theory can be developed.

The same method that I argue other qualitative researchers should use I have used in the writing of this book. The dialogue between tradition and innovation reflexively applies my own argument that new interpretations do not arise *de novo*, uninfluenced by preexisting interpretations. Similarly, new methods, and approaches to qualitative data analysis do not arise *de novo*, uninfluenced by preexisting traditions and approaches to data analysis. The challenge for qualitative research is to bring established traditions and innovative methods into dialogue. Again, there are two main mistakes. Some qualitative researchers ignore, or overzealously refute, the innovations currently being explored in qualitative methods. Other researchers appear to adopt these innovations uncritically, losing sight of the value of established methods. Actively engaging established traditions in debate with recent innovations leads to a research practice that is more rigorous, methodologically robust, theoretically sophisticated and politically relevant.

To advocate dialogue between tradition and innovation is to take a political position in the ongoing debate about the nature of qualitative research. As Bauman notes in the quote at the beginning of this introduction, it is impossible to be neutral or disengaged. My preferences and predilections are clear in the topics I focus on, and those I overlook, in my choice of examples, and in the commentary I provide on them. More generally, this book is an argument for the ongoing relevance and usefulness of qualitative methods that are still routinely undervalued, despite their growing influence.

At the heart of insightful qualitative research is a well-established dialogue between ideas and observations, between theory and data, between interpretation and action. Similarly, at the heart of this book is a dialogue between tradition and innovation, established and experimental methods, modernist and postmodernist theory, time-honoured writing styles and new writing styles. In this dialogue I describe some of the diversity of available methods of data analysis, with a sensitivity to their strengths, weakness and appropriate applications. This book is not an encyclopaedic classification of qualitative data analysis methods. Rather, it is a contribution to the ongoing dialogue between academics, researchers and other practitioners of qualitative methods. I have learnt much from what others have already written, spoken and performed. I hope that others will find this contribution similarly useful.

The organisation of the book

The book contains six chapters that each focus on different aspects of the interpretive process. It is not necessary to read each chapter in sequence, although most of the later chapters draw on the theoretical arguments developed in Chapter 1, so it may be useful to read that chapter first.

Grounded theory and symbolic interactionism are the theoretical orientations that have informed qualitative methods since the 1960s. However, recently a number of theoretical innovations have unsettled many of the primary assumptions of qualitative researchers. Chapter 1 reviews both the traditional methodologies and recent innovations such as postmodernism, feminist standpoint epistemology and hermeneutics. I argue that each tradition provides a different approach to qualitative research that should be valued for its contribution. In particular, although postmodernism has disrupted the naive inductivist assumptions of traditional method-ologies, this does not lead to relativism, but to an epistemology, and methodology, that must explicitly acknowledge the situated and political nature of its contribution to ongoing theoretical and policy debates. In particular, I argue for a hermeneutic approach to quali-tative data analysis. Hermeneutics is the theory of interpretation. It theorises the relationship between our own pre-existing interpreta-tions and the interpretation of the texts and people we are studying. Hermeneutic practices are interpretive practices. The craft of the qualitative researcher is a hermeneutic craft. This book is, in many ways, a working out of the hermeneutic practices of qualitative researchers.

Rather than seeing qualitative methods informed by postmod-ernism and hermeneutics as antagonistic to an applied focus, I argue in Chapter 2 that a sophisticated qualitative methodology must explicitly engage political implications. The chapter begins with a review of the different ways in which qualitative research can be relevant to the policy process, and then moves to an examination of how published research has actually influenced, or failed to influ-ence, public policy. The second half of the chapter moves through a discussion of feminist and participatory action research to an examination of the nature of rigour. I argue that an explicit commit-ment to acknowledging the political dimensions of all research does not necessarily lead to research driven by political agendas. Rather, it results in more rigorous, useful and ethical analysis.

The task of interpreting qualitative data begins during data collection. While I do not discuss the various methodologies of qualitative data collection in detail, Chapter 3 examines some of the techniques that can be employed during data collection to initiate data analysis during this early stage of the research. Team meetings, participant review of transcripts, coding during data collection, journals and memos, and issues related to sampling are all reviewed. The chapter finishes with a discussion of the value, and dangers, of including participants not simply as sources of data but as co-researchers, contributing to various aspects of the data analysis process.

Coding data and interpreting text (the title of Chapter 4) suggests the tension between the traditional focus on coding patterns in the data, and the more recent focus on interpreting the meaning of texts through relating them to more general theoretical frameworks and cultural processes. The analytic strategies of content analysis and thematic analysis or grounded theory revolve around the practical task of how to code data. The analytic strategies of cultural studies focus more on theoretical interpretation of the text in relation to more general cultural and political processes. Narrative analysis draws from both these genres but focuses on the systematic analysis of the structure of the text. Qualitative research influenced by cultural studies is typically theoretically and politically sophisticated, but often methodologically naive. Social research, in comparison, is often methodologically sophisticated, but often politically naive. I attempt to place these two traditions alongside one another and in dialogue with each other. I hope that by doing so these two traditions can learn more from one another and, while remaining distinct, both work towards more sophisticated practices, theory and politics.

Computer-assisted qualitative data analysis (CAQDAS) is increasingly utilised by qualitative researchers. Chapter 5 examines published accounts of how researchers have used CAQDAS software, focusing on both the advantages and disadvantages. CAQDAS software can significantly improve some types of qualitative research with particular sorts of data, particular types of analytic strategies, and adequate time and resources. Computer-assisted analysis is not always the best choice, and this chapter examines when and why this might be the case. It then reviews how researchers have utilised CAQDAS software in the analysis process, with particular attention to both the potential benefits and problems associated with the use of such software.

The final Chapter 6 discusses the writing process, pointing out that this is as much a part of the analytic and interpretive process as is data collection. The chapter again works the tension between a discussion of traditional practices, such as different writing styles and the importance of illustrative examples, and a discussion of recent developments including experimental writing styles such as poetry and performance and the inclusion of researchers' personal experiences in research reports. The chapter concludes by recounting the political and ethical dimensions that should be taken into account during the writing process.

Acknowledgements

This book reflects my educational and employment history. My undergraduate and honours education was completed in sociology at the University of Tasmania in the late 1980s in a department mainly influenced by Anglo-American theory and methodology. The qualitative method I learnt was thematic analysis and grounded theory. My PhD was completed in sociology at La Trobe University during the early 1990s, a department profoundly influenced by European social theory. I read social theory like a hungry child. After a year lecturing I worked for two years at the National Centre in HIV Social Research at La Trobe University. This was a baptism into the political realities of applied research. I am now back in sociology at the University of Tasmania, teaching qualitative research methods. The balancing act in my employment and educational history between grounded theory, social theory and social policy is reflected in the book. I do not pretend to be developing a 'new synthesis'. I fully recognise that each tradition and methodology has its place, and its distinctive value. However, I remain convinced that each tradition could benefit significantly from a more open dialogue with the other traditions of qualitative research. I would not have reached this position without the challenges, dialogue and debate of my colleagues at these institutions.

In particular I would like to thank Professor Allan Kellehear, who was a wise and insightful supervisor and has continued as a friend and adviser. I would also like to acknowledge the influence of Dr Pranee Liamputtong Rice, with whom I have previously collaborated on another qualitative text, and whose 'standpoint' was a breath of fresh air in a world dominated by old white Anglo men. My partner Susi Ezzy read parts of the book, and talked about many more of them.

Theory and data: a hermeneutic approach

> Understanding comes not from the subject who thinks, but from the
> other that addresses me. This other . . . is this voice that awakens one
> to vigilance, to being questioned in the conversation that we are.
> (Risser 1997: 208)

> What is of critical importance, therefore, is the way in which those
> statements are made sense of, that is, interpreted. Here lies the
> ultimate responsibility of the researcher. The comfortable assumption
> that it is the reliability and accuracy of the methodologies being used
> that will ascertain the validity of the outcomes of research, thereby
> reducing the researcher's responsibility to a technical matter, is
> rejected. (Ang 1996: 47)

As a teenager I attended an after-hours class to learn New Testament Greek. My teacher wanted to know why I was interested in
Greek. I replied: 'I want to know about truth'. I thought I could find
the truth through an understanding of the original language of the
New Testament. The question of truth has haunted me since that
time. What is this thing called 'truth'? Is there a truth to be discovered that applies for all time and everywhere? Or is there no such
thing as absolute truth, and is everything relative? Driven by the
fear of extreme relativism and the need for certainty I searched for
various forms of transcendent truths. Truths that I could live by
with absolute confidence. I tried fundamentalist religion, alternative subcultures, dedicating myself to a career and the certainty of
logical science. However, the more I read, the more people I met,

the more I experienced, the more I became convinced that this is a false dichotomy. It is not a choice between absolute truth and no truth at all. Rather, truth is always historical, cultural and socially created. Historically and culturally located truths still provide a guide for living, but the person who recognises their historical and cultural location is more willing to listen to, and respect the voice and experience—the 'truth'—of other people. Between the extremes of absolute truth and no truth is the lived reality of half-worked-through truths that shape our daily lives.

In this chapter I describe qualitative data analysis, drawing on the theoretical perspectives of hermeneutics, postmodernism, feminist standpoint epistemology and symbolic interactionist grounded theory. Qualitative research drawing on these perspectives does not attempt to arrive at absolute laws that apply to all people everywhere. However, neither does it give up the attempt to make generalisations and theories. There are qualitative researchers who still advocate the extremes of, on the one hand, trying to identify universal laws of human behaviour and, on the other hand, claiming that there are no certainties and that everything is completely culturally and historically relative. Somewhere in between is a more modest approach, which recognises the limited nature of theory but still values its usefulness. This is the approach developed here.

This chapter begins by examining the role of theory in shaping the process of interpreting data. People interpret data all the time in their everyday lives. Interpreting data as part of a qualitative research project is a special case, although similar processes operate in both instances. The chapter then reviews symbolic interactionist-grounded theory, postmodernism, feminist standpoint epistemology and hermeneutics. Each of these is an important theoretical perspective that has influenced contemporary qualitative data analysis. I examine how these approaches have dealt with the role of theory in qualitative research, along the way discussing some of the central insights of each perspective and providing illustrations from published research.

What is theory?

A theory is a statement about relationships between variables or concepts (Kellehear 1993). A theoretical perspective is a set of theories, and is sometimes called a paradigm or tradition. For example, we may have a theory that women are more likely to be dangerous drivers than men. The theory states that there is a relationship between the gender of the driver and the likelihood of the car being involved in an accident. Similarly, within the more general theoretical perspective of symbolic interactionism, labelling theory argues that deviance is constituted by social groups (Becker 1963). Labelling theory states that there is a relationship between the stigmatisation of particular individual characteristics and more general group processes that constitute particular characteristics as deviant. For example, Heckert and Best (1997) analyse the way in which group stereotypes of red hair as deviant influence the socialisation of children with red hair.

Qualitative research methods are particularly good at examining and developing theories that deal with the role of meanings and interpretations. The theory that women are more dangerous drivers is not about meanings, and it is easily tested using statistical analysis of quantitative data. However, the theory that deviant identities are a product of particular sorts of social experiences focuses on the process of interpretation and the construction of red hair, for example, as having a deviant meaning. This theory is not easily tested using statistical methods, and studies that examine the theory require a qualitative methodology that focuses on meanings and interpretation.

The focus on meaning creates a distinctive problem for the qualitative researcher. Meaning is not a thing or a substance but an activity. This makes meanings difficult to grasp. Meanings are constantly changing, and are produced and reproduced in each social situation with slightly different nuances and significances depending on the nature of the context as a whole. Qualitative research in general, and hermeneutics in particular, engages with this linguistic uncertainty and uses linguistic techniques such as analogies and metaphors to draw conclusions about the meaning of particular social events or texts.

Theories shape how people explain what they observe. I can still remember my father exclaiming 'Women drivers!' when he observed a car being driven in a dangerous manner. Incorrect theories still shape how people interpret the world. Thomas made precisely this point when he argued that 'if people define situations as real, they are real in their consequences' (1928: 584). In this case, the theory is incorrect. Even when the differences in distances driven and times of driving are taken into account, men are still more likely than women to have an accident while driving a car (Berger 1986).

This has important implications for the practice of qualitative research.

Theories shape both how qualitative data analysis is conducted and what is noticed when qualitative data are analysed. This is the case whether the theories are correct or not. The difference with qualitative data analysis, however, is that the analyst is continually making a systematic effort to identify these sources of bias and to analyse the data in such a way as to modify and reconceptualise their theory. Research often begins with a general theoretical orientation but then, through empirical observation, specifies in more detail the nature and character of the process described in the theory. Heckert and Best (1997), for example, begin with the general observation that red hair is stigmatising, but through their interviews with people with red hair find that the main source of this stigma is peer relations during adolescence. Parents do not stigmatise children with red hair, and when these children reach adulthood red hair is transformed into a valued aspect of individual personality.

Theories describe general patterns of social behaviour, but theories are not absolute rules or laws. They are always a product of particular historical and cultural situations. It would be possible, for example, for a government to begin a campaign to encourage men to be safe drivers. Alternatively, young women might develop a gang culture that values driving very fast. If either of these things happened, women could become more dangerous drivers than men. While society does change, it typically changes slowly. Theories are historically and culturally located, but are still useful as generalisations to describe and analyse behaviour within relevant cultural and historical periods.

Howard Becker (1963) studied marijuana use in the late 1950s in America, and his analysis is a classic demonstration of both qualitative methods and the type of theory developed using qualitative research. His study has since been repeated and supported (Hirsch et al. 1990). Becker's main theoretical orientation was that of symbolic interactionism. This emphasises the influence of meanings, or the symbolic significances of people's experiences. Specifically, Becker argued that getting high from smoking marijuana is a socially learned experience. A smoker must learn three things: (1) to smoke the drug in a way that will produce real effects; (2) to recognise the effects and connect them with drug use; and (3) to enjoy the sensations he or she perceives. Popular understandings suggest that the effects of marijuana are biologically produced—that if you smoke and inhale you will get high, or become paranoid (some people have adverse reactions to marijuana use). However, while biology is part of the process, Becker shows that the likelihood of a person defining the experience they have after smoking marijuana as pleasurable 'depends on the degree of the individual's participation with other users' (Becker 1963: 56). In other words, Becker's theory is that there is a relationship between experiencing the effects of marijuana use as pleasurable and the degree of interaction with other people who already use marijuana. Becker's specific theory draws on the more general theoretical perspective of symbolic interactionism that emphasises the role of meanings and interpretations in shaping what people do and their experiences.

In summary, theory produced as part of qualitative data analysis is typically a statement or a set of statements about relationships between variables or concepts that focus on meanings and interpretations. Theories influence how qualitative analysis is conducted. The qualitative researcher attempts to elaborate or develop a theory to provide a more useful understanding of the phenomenon. The focus on meanings makes qualitative research difficult to do well, because meanings are more 'slippery' than quantitative statistics. Meanings are easily disputed, more malleable, and manipulated. However, despite these difficulties, theories that focus on meanings provide rich rewards in explaining and understanding human action.

A theory is a set of ideas. Theories are written down and talked about. How do we know that this or that theory is right or wrong? How do we know that a theory is true? Does a theory accurately represent what is happening in the world? Are theories already part of what is happening in the world anyway? What if we start with an incorrect theory: will this stop us from seeing data that might contradict it? Should we start research by examining existing theories, or should we start with a 'clean slate'? The rest of this chapter examines these issues through a discussion of the role of some of the central theories that have influenced qualitative research.

Interpretation in everyday life

The construction of theories in qualitative data analysis follows the same sort of process as the construction of interpretive frameworks in everyday life. A theory is a particular type of interpretive framework. Qualitative data analysis, of course, involves a number of systematic procedures and techniques for developing and testing theories, and these are discussed in detail later in the book. The interpretive process involves an ongoing cycle in which preexisting interpretive frameworks shape how people make sense of their experiences, and these experiences, in turn, shape the development of new interpretive frameworks.

In everyday life, 'understanding involves active, unconscious, processes by which presented information is combined with relevant pre-understandings (i.e., knowledge stored in long term memory)' (Turnbull 1986: 141). There is no reason to suggest that social science researchers should be exempt from this process. To make this observation is simply to apply the phenomenological or hermeneutic insight reflexively: People's preexisting meanings and interpretive frameworks are the dominant influences on what people do and observe. That is to say, an epistemology that makes a radical separation between fact and theory does not deal adequately with the theory-dependent nature of data. Or, to put it another way, the circle of interpretation and experience works for both the people we study and for the people who do the study. Grounded theory is one of the dominant influences on qualitative methods. The next section examines the role of theory in grounded

Figure 1.1: Interpretation in everyday life

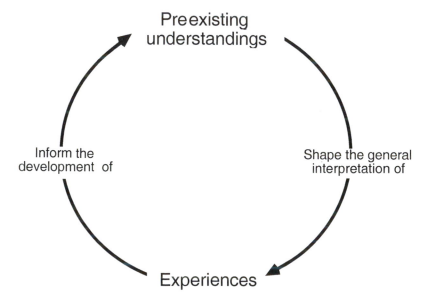

Preexisting understandings

Inform the development of

Shape the general interpretation of

Experiences

theory, contrasting this with other understandings of the role of theory in qualitative research.

Symbolic interactionism and grounded theory

Grounded theory was developed by Barney Glaser and Anselm Strauss in the 1960s, drawing on the symbolic interactionist theoretical perspective (Glaser & Strauss 1967). Strauss is one of the leading theorists of symbolic interactionism (Maines 1991). While early symbolic interactionist studies had developed theory in a 'grounded' way, Glaser and Strauss (1967) provided a clear description of the method of grounded theory generation. Grounded theory is 'grounded' in data and observation. Glaser and Strauss argued that data gathering should not be influenced by preconceived theories. Rather, systematic data collection and analysis should lead into theory. Grounded theory was developed, in part, as a reaction to the deductive model of theory generation that was dominant in the United States in the 1960s.

Glaser and Strauss (1965a, 1965b), provide a classic grounded theory study of dying. They identify three temporal aspects of dying: '(1) legitimating when the passage occurs, (2) announcing the passage to others, and (3) co-ordinating the passage' (Glaser & Strauss 1965a: 48). Their theory is that the experience of dying is primarily shaped by the temporal characteristics of dying. In their appendix, Glaser and Strauss describe how their theory of dying was developed through careful observation during fieldwork: 'Fieldwork allows researchers to plunge into social settings where the important events (about which they will develop theory) are going on "naturally"' (1956b: 288). While some general concerns with death expectations shaped their data collection, they emphasise that the theory was developed through empirical observation and data collection. That is to say, it is 'grounded theory', although they did not use the exact phrase until their later text of that name (Glaser & Strauss 1967). I will discuss grounded theory in more detail after a short discussion of deductive theory building.

Deductive theory building

Grounded theory explicitly rejects the 'logico-deductive' method of theory building and verification. The logico-deductive method starts with an abstract theory, logically deduces some implications, formulates some hypotheses, and then develops experiments or tests to verify or falsify the truth of the hypotheses. The logico-deductive method builds down from abstract preexisting theory. What actually happens—the events of everyday life, or data—becomes important only as part of a test of hypotheses logically deduced from more general theory.

A deductively derived theory is one that is logically derived from more general principles. For example, functionalist theories of the family argue that the important aspects of the family are those that serve to maintain the social order. A functionalist study of the family using a logico-deductive method would examine the data only to see whether it supports this theory. Functionalist studies of the family point to its significance in regulating sexual behaviour, reproducing members of society, socialising new members, caring for and pro-tecting vulnerable members, and placing new social members in appropriate roles (Parsons & Bales 1955). Each of these is an aspect of maintaining and reproducing a stable and ordered society. The deductively derived expectations of functionalist theory shaped both what was observed and how it was observed. The family may perform those functions identified by Parsons and Bales. However,

Figure 1.2: Deductive theory building

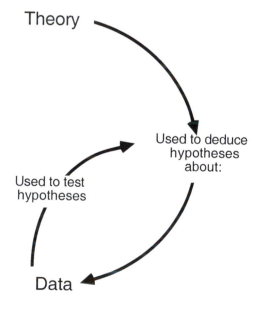

to limit the analysis of contemporary families to these dimensions results in a narrow view and a limited theory. It ignores, for example, the way in which families serve to reproduce inequalities, and disturb social order. When theory generation is limited to deductive methodologies it restricts the possible interpretations of the observed data. Deductive theorising is useful, but it is limited because it typically does not produce new understandings and new theoretical explanations that may contradict the initial theory.

Some researchers have a great deal invested in their preexisting theories and misuse qualitative methods to support their theories. Johnson (1999) makes a case that Parse, a leading nursing researcher, utilises a form of qualitative research to verify her preexisting theory. Johnson claims that the evidence presented in support of Parse's theory is 'tenuous', and there is no consideration of alternative explanations. If Johnson's analysis is correct, then this is a clear example of precisely the sort of problem identified by the early grounded theorists, where data are forced to fit a theory. Central to grounded theory is an attempt to allow the data to speak, or for the researcher to engage with what the data have to say. As Johnson succinctly summarises: 'some researchers use what they inappropriately understand as "qualitative" methods to reproduce their own theories and ideas, often without a serious relation to what data are presented' (1999: 71).

Strauss and Corbin argue that 'it makes no sense to start with received theories or variables (categories)' (1990: 50). This rejection is consistent with grounded theory's emphasis on the inductive nature of theory building. However, on closer examination, the concern of Strauss and Corbin is not to reject deductive theory generation completely. Rather, grounded theorists object to the typical way in which deductively derived theory is brought into relationship with the data: 'it makes no sense to start with received theories or variables (categories) *because* these are likely to inhibit or impede the development of new theoretical formulations, unless of course your purpose is to open these up and to find new meanings in them' (Strauss & Corbin 1990: 50, emphasis added).

That is to say, their objection is not to the use of preexisting theory *per se*, but to the way in which it might influence the research process: 'it would hinder progress and stifle creativity' (Strauss & Corbin 1990: 53). Grounded theory does make use of preexisting theory, but the early grounded theorists had to make a strong case against preexisting theory because of the 'absurdly

9

restricted and inadequate vision' of verificationist methodology that dominated American sociology at the time of the development of grounded theory in the 1960s (Gerson 1991: 300).

Simplistic inductive theory building

Some grounded theory texts seem to advocate a simplistic inductive methodology for generating theory. Glaser, for example, argues that 'the first step in gaining theoretical sensitivity is to enter the research setting with as few predetermined ideas as possible' (1978: 3). Glaser seems to suggest that researchers should not read the literature or develop hypotheses before entering the field. Glaser appears to advocate a naive form of inductive theorising.

In line with the anti-deductivist tone of the main methodological texts, the *practice* of grounded theory also often appears to proceed on the basis of an assumption that the researcher is a *tabula rasa*, who will absorb and understand the meanings of the subjects of the research unfettered by any of the researcher's previous understandings. Minichiello et al. (1990) provide a revealing insight into exactly this process when they describe a grounded theory research project in the following way:

> The important point here is that Legatt's conclusions rested on the views, attitudes and definitions of her informants. She had no formal hypothesis, and kept her hunches at the back of her mind while she listened and tried to comprehend the everyday reality of her informants. Her hunches were developed throughout the research, and when she nearly completed the project these contributed to hypotheses or theories for further testing (Minichiello et al. 1990: 102).

I think Minichiello and his associates underestimate the influence of preexisting theory on the research process. Hunches cannot be and should not be kept 'at the back of your mind'. Rather, the first step towards dealing with the influence of preconceptions is not to deny or hide them, but to formally state them. As argued earlier, all data are theory driven. The point is not to pretend that they are not, or to force the data into the theory. Rather, the researcher should enter into an ongoing simultaneous process of deduction and induction, of theory building, testing and rebuilding.

For most grounded theorists, the problem is not the existence of prior hypotheses, but how these interact with the research process.

Figure 1.3: Simplistic inductive theory building

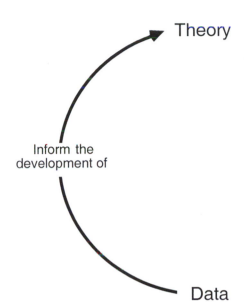

Theory

Inform the
development of

Data

As Strauss and Corbin (1990) point out, literature reviews are often an important initial stage in developing grounded theory. Deductively derived hypotheses are a problem when they are associated with a researcher's commitment to a more general theoretical scheme. This commitment constrains what the researcher studies and prevents the researcher from discovering new understandings of the phenomenon under investigation. Whether they come from preexisting theory or from previous experience, all researchers have preconceptions that shape what they see when conducting research. The main point of grounded theory is not to avoid these preconceptions, but to actively work to prevent preconceptions from narrowing what is observed and theorised.

The dangers identified by grounded theory are twofold: either, through *overemphasising theoretical deductions*, the researcher will not be prepared to reformulate theories in response to new evidence or an *overemphasis on inductive theory* grounded in 'data' will result in a failure to be explicit about the preexisting theoretical sources of ideas.

Grounded theory recognises the influence of preexisting theories. Preexisting theory sensitises the researcher to particular issues and aspects of the phenomenon being studied. However, grounded theory searches for dimensions of the experience not covered by preexisting theory. Grounded theory inductively generates new theory through careful and repeated observation. These inductively generated theories are then, in turn, used to shape further research, and their implications are tested against the observed data.

Grounded theory: a sophisticated model

The more sophisticated uses of grounded theory draw on both inductive and deductive methods of theory generation. In contrast to simplistic deduction, grounded theory argues that theory can be built up through careful observation of the social world: 'A grounded theory is one that is inductively derived from the study of the phenomenon it represents. That is, theory is discovered, developed, and provisionally verified through systematic data collection and analysis of data pertaining to that phenomenon' (Strauss & Corbin 1990: 23). According to the methods of grounded theory, concepts, categories and themes are identified and developed while the research is being conducted. In many ways grounded theory is a reaction against the natural science model of research method that always begins with hypotheses to be tested. Rather, grounded theorists begin by identifying some important issues that guide the collection of data. Theory is built up from observation. Observations are not selected to test a theory. Theory is 'grounded' in data.

However, in contrast to simplistic induction, many grounded theorists emphasise the role of preexisting theory in sensitising the researcher to orienting questions that need to be examined during the research. The task of the grounded theorist is to allow deductions from preexisting theory to suggest specific research problems and foci, but the researcher must not allow this preexisting theory to constrain what is noticed. The grounded theorist uses deductively derived theory, but also examines questions and issues beyond what is suggested by deductively derived theory.

A good example of this process is provided by Karp and his associates (1998), who develop a grounded theory of the experience of leaving home in anticipation of attending university or, as they term it, 'college'. After interviewing 23 students who were about to leave home to attend university, they identify four aspects

Figure 1.4: Grounded theory: a sophisticated model

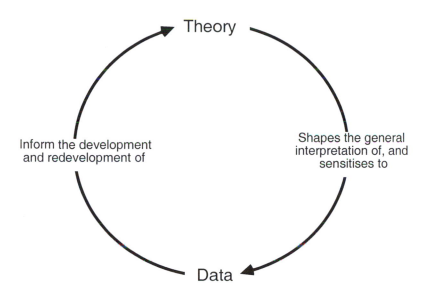

of the experience: 'Students anticipated change, planned to affirm certain identities, imagined creating new identities, and contemplated discovering unanticipated identities' (Karp et al. 1998: 253). These aspects of anticipating leaving home are inductively grounded in the data of the interviews that were conducted. They are not deduced from a general theory. However, the symbolic interactionist emphasis on meanings and identity clearly shaped the sorts of questions that the study examined. Karp et al. describe clearly how this preexisting theory guided the method of their study: 'Consistent with the logic of grounded theory, this study did not begin with any explicit hypotheses to be tested. Instead, we began with broad sensitizing questions about the meaning of going to college and leaving home for both children and their parents' (1998: 255).

Induction, deduction, abduction

Grounded theory developed out of the pragmatist tradition of social philosophy, including C.S. Peirce, G.H. Mead and W. James. Peirce's (1965) theory of abduction provides the philosophical background to the processes that are involved in grounded theory. Peirce distinguished between deductive, inductive and abductive theory generation. Deductive theories are logically derived from more general propositions. Inductive theories are built up from observation through systemic empirical data collection. Deduction moves from a general rule to specific cases. Induction moves from specific cases to the general law. *Abduction*, however, produced a form of synthetic knowledge that introduced new ideas through the generation of new hypotheses. Abduction is like a 'creative leap of the mind', where people all of a sudden understand how a particular event fits into a broader picture or explanation (Davis 1972: 4). Peirce suggests that abduction occurs 'where we find some curious circumstance, which could be explained by the supposition that it was a case of a certain general rule, and thereupon adopt that supposition' (1965: 624, vol. 2). This hypothesis is then tested by deductive logic and inductive empirical comparisons. In other words, preexisting theories are not used to determine how observation is done, but they inform the process of observing through suggesting, during the process of abduction, general social processes or 'rules' that may apply to particular observations. These hypotheses are then tested through more rigorous deduction and induction.

Abduction makes imaginative leaps to new theories to explain observations. The difference between induction and abduction is that abduction makes this leap to a general theory without having completely empirically demonstrated all the required steps. Peirce differentiated between *induction* 'which depends upon our confidence that a run of one kind of experience will not be changed or cease without some indication before it ceases' and *abduction* 'which depends on our hope, sooner or later, to guess at the conditions under which a given kind of phenomenon will present itself' (quoted in Sebeok 1983: 2).

Peirce's theory of abduction bears many similarities to, and some significant differences from, the practice of detective work by Sherlock Holmes (Eco 1983; Sebeok 1983; Shank 2001). Holmes was the master of abduction. Holmes compares possible explanations against a few facts and then through an abductive leap arrives at the larger picture that explains what has happened. He is always supremely confident, and never makes a mistake. This is, of course, a privilege that Conan Doyle has that research social scientists do not! However, in 'real life', suggests Eco, 'detectives commit more frequently (or more frequently visible) errors than scientists'. This is because detectives are rewarded for charging the criminal even though all the evidence may not be in, whereas 'scientists are socially rewarded for their patience in testing their abductions' (Eco 1983: 220).

Abductively generated theories may be, or initially appear to be, inconsistent with existing, or obvious explanations. That is to say, abductive reasoning is prepared to accept a certain level of inconsistency and ambiguity in the analysis. As Eco puts it, one of the characteristics of abduction is 'the courage of challenging without further tests the basic fallibilism that governs human knowledge' (1983: 220). More generally, Peirce's conception of abduction provides an important concept for analysing the role of indeterminacy in linguistics and more general social theory (Melrose 1995).

For Peirce, the discovery of new understandings did not occur either through simplistic deduction alone, or through simplistic induction alone. Rather, abduction followed by induction and deduction involved a complex process of inference, insight, empirical observation and logical reasoning. This shuttling back and forth between general propositions and empirical data is central to the process of discovery. Abductive reasoning is an important part of the cycle of theory building and data collection in grounded theory. Abductive reasoning allows for new theories to be developed. However, these theories are then subjected to an ongoing cycle of deductive examination and inductive confirmation through further research and data collection.

Postmodernism

Postmodernism is a complex set of ideas. It is complex both in the sense that it is difficult to grasp and in the sense that there are a number of varieties of postmodernism, many of which argue for a variety of different approaches that are sometimes contradictory. Nonetheless, postmodernist theory has provided a major stimulus to the analysis of the role of theory in qualitative research, and its contribution deserves careful analysis.

Denzin suggests that what puts the qualitative studies of symbolic interactionists outside a postmodernist project is their insistence that 'there is an empirical world out there that must be respected' (1992: 120). However, Denzin's point, as I understand it, is not that the empirical world does not exist. To 'seriously question' the 'ontological status' of the empirical world, as Denzin suggests, is not to deny it but to problematise it. These are very different things. Some analysts seem to think that the problematising of empirical reality means denying its existence. However, the point is to examine the interpretive process through which empirical and subjective realities are created.

It is easy to criticise postmodernism as an extreme form of relativism. Huber, for example, simply asserts that: 'Postmodernists are complete relativists who see science as an intellectual device to further the ends of those paying for research rather than a way to discover truth about the universe'(1995: 205). The problem with this assertion is that it is half true. Some postmodernists do make the sort of claims that Huber suggests, or at least they appear to; whereas others do not. The more sophisticated postmodernists are not attempting to deny the existence of reality—they are attempting to demonstrate that interpretation is a complex process, and that there is no final or absolute truth.

It is easy to criticise postmodernism for not believing in 're-ality'. For example, Farberman, who does not like postmodernism, criticises Fee (1992), who values postmodernism, claiming that Fee says 'there is no empirical world out there aside from what is created by ideologically suffused language' (Farberman 1992: 375). However, Fee's comments are more qualified, suggesting that postmodernism provides 'sufficient reason to rethink many of our taken-for-granted assumptions about the empirical world *out there*' (1992: 368, original emphasis). The implication of arguing that language has nothing to do with empirical objects is quite different from suggesting that we should rethink our knowledge of empirical objects in the light of the complexity of the interpretive process.

Some empirical studies influenced by postmodernism and cultural studies do appear to claim that there is no reality apart from subjective perceptions. Linde, for example, argues that the actual facts of a person's life are irrelevant to her study: 'all we can ever work with is texts of one sort or another' (Linde 1993: 14). While Linde is partially correct, in the sense that all action is textually mediated, she tends towards a closed semanticism that fails to deal with exigencies of practical action. Sceptical analyses of the role of language, of which Linde's work is an example, set up a false dichotomy. Either language is transparent and reflects lived experience accurately, or it is a distorting screen that always projects experience out of its own categories. If language is viewed as unavoidably distorting understanding, and there are no criteria that can be used to judge an explanation's correctness, then all explanations of events are 'equally legitimate and adequate' (Spence 1988: 68). This understanding typically rests on an argument for the underlying disorder of 'reality'. 'Reality' is conceived to be indescribable, and there is a radical disjunction between reality and narrative. Trigger describes this as 'extreme relativism': 'Extreme relativists deny that there can be any evidential grounds for assessing the relative merits of different interpretations of human behaviour' (1989: 78). This form of radical postmodernism is represented in Figure 1.5.

More famously, one of Derrida's most quoted statements is 'there is nothing outside the text' (1976: 158). Lucy argues that it is a significant misunderstanding to deduce that 'the statement "there is nothing outside the text" . . . [means] that there is no truth, no reality, no history, no actual flesh-and-blood people in the world' (1995: 1). Many commentators seem to have drawn this conclusion from Derrida's statements, and Lucy is right to highlight that this is a misunderstanding of Derrida. Derrida is arguing that language and interpretation are central to all human experience. However, when taken to its extreme logical conclusion this leads to a form of textual solipsism, where theory seems to bear no relationship to the events of lived experience. The problem for most postmodernists is that they convincingly demonstrate that language and interpretation are central to human experience, but do not provide a convincing answer to the problem of how to differentiate 'true' from 'false' accounts of the world.

Deconstruction and postmodernism take the lid off the myth of objective knowledge, but many postmodernists do not provide a convincing response to the charge of relativism. This point is taken up in Chapter 2, where I review the problematic nature of the political and ethical implications of postmodernist theory: 'Although the later Derrida protests that deconstruction is not sealed off from the outer world of acting and does not close us up in "language as in a cave", one has difficulty squaring this with certain statements in his early work' (Kearny 1999: 148).

Researchers arguing against postmodernism and for traditional, modernist, research methods are often doing so in an attempt to avoid dealing with the role of interpretation in shaping the research process (Denzin 1996a). Some people who criticise postmodernism, such as Huber (1995), are using postmodernist relativism as a 'straw man'. Rather than engaging with the problem of interpretation that the postmodernists raise, these forms of argument simply try to discredit postmodernism, preferring to ignore the issue of the historical and situated nature of knowledge. This line of approach typically argues for a return to deductive theory building and the application of natural science methods to the social sciences.

Theory building can still be conducted within a postmodernist frame using qualitative research (Daly, K. 1997). Kvale, for example, argues that a 'moderate' postmodernist position does not lead to the conclusion of extreme relativism. Rather, 'while rejecting the notion of a universal truth, it [moderate postmodernism] accepts the possibility of specific, local, personal and community forms of truth with a focus on daily life and local narrative' (Kvale 1995: 21). These moderate forms of postmodernist theory have much in common with standpoint epistemology and hermeneutics, discussed below.

Postmodernist qualitative researchers have demonstrated that the traditional forms of qualitative research, and their conception of

Figure 1.5: Radical postmodernism

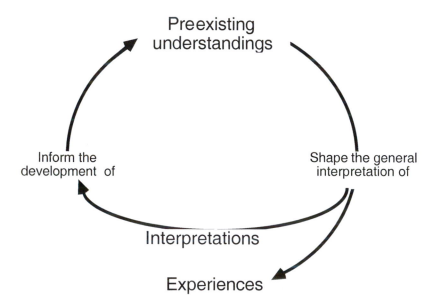

theory in particular, are deeply problematic (Denzin 1997; Clough 1992; Richardson 1991). At the most general level, postmodernists have pointed out that research is not an objective enterprise but is fundamentally influenced by theory. Specifically, postmodernists have asked questions that focus on: the role of the researcher in producing the research; the location of the research within more general social and political structures; the limited and historically located nature of all research; and the problematic, changing and inconsistent nature of reality. While the researcher may not agree with the answers that particular postmodernists have provided to these questions about how qualitative data analysis is conducted, the questions themselves can no longer be ignored. I deal with each of these points in detail throughout this book. Denzin sums up the argument succinctly when he says that the qualitative researcher 'can no longer presume to be able to present an objective, uncontested account of the other's experiences' (1997: xiii).

Ronai's (1998) reflections on her research among erotic dancers provides a clear analysis of the influence of Derrida's postmodernist theory on the analysis of qualitative data. As a participant observer, Ronai was both a dancer and a researcher. However, this distinction is problematic for Ronai: 'If I explore the "play of differences" (Derrida) between the two, I deconstruct my experience by decentring the researcher identity' (1998: 419). Ronai does not simply replace the researcher identity with the dancer identity, but attempts to play the two identities against one another: 'Because meaning is always subject to reinterpretation, there is no final dividing line for a binary construct like dancer/researcher' (Ronai 1998: 420). Her point is to explicitly examine the way the researcher participates in the research process and influences the construction of the events she is describing.

One elegant use of Foucault's (1977) postmodernist theory is Chris Grey's (1994) study of accountancy careers. Instead of a focus on the details and influences on individual career choices, characteristic of most studies of careers, Grey's Foucauldian theoretical orientation towards 'panoptic techniques of disciplinary power' focuses on 'the concept of career as an organising and regulative principle' (1994: 481). This means that he examines the political and control functions of the 'career' aimed at ensuring the compliance of accountants who feel they must work hard, disciplining themselves to conform to the requirements of the firm. In the context of this chapter the most important implication of Grey's

19

study is that by adopting a postmodernist theory, Grey is able to question and problematise the taken-for-granted realities of the people he is studying. He shows how their 'realities' are produced through particular discourses of power and disciplinary techniques.

Feminist standpoint methodology

Feminist standpoint epistemologies began as an opposition movement to modernist positivism and deductivist theorising. An epistemology is a way of knowing, or a theory of how we know things about the world. Feminist standpoint epistemologies reject the modernist assumption that there is a single ideal knower and that he (it is typically a male) can know or describe one true and final correct representation or reality. Rather, they argue that knowledge is always situated, and what is known is influenced by the shared experiences and political orientations of the standpoint of the person who knows. All knowledge is knowledge from where a person stands. Standpoint epistemologists reject the implicit and hidden white male standpoint of mainstream science. Masculine mainstream science has presumed that this male standpoint is the only 'objective' standpoint. Feminist standpoint epistemology disputes this traditional masculine picture of science, 'replacing it with a clear emancipatory commitment to knowledge from the standpoint of women's experience and feminist theory' (McLennan 1995: 392).

There is a wide variety of feminist standpoint epistemologies. Dorothy Smith's (1974) first essay on standpoint theory was broadly influential, although a number of authors developed similar ideas independently, including Harstock (1983) and Collins (1990). Dorothy Smith (1997) argues that Harding (1986) identified and grouped together these previously independent 'standpoint theorists'.

Linking social categories to politics is central to the approach of standpoint theory: 'Race, gender, social class, ethnicity, age, and sexuality are not descriptive categories of identity applied to individuals. Instead, these elements of social structure emerge as fundamental devices that foster inequality resulting in groups' (Collins 1997: 375). Standpoint epistemology takes these shared political and social experiences and works out both an account of experience and an approach to politics from the standpoint of these groups.

Figure 1.6: Standpoint epistemology

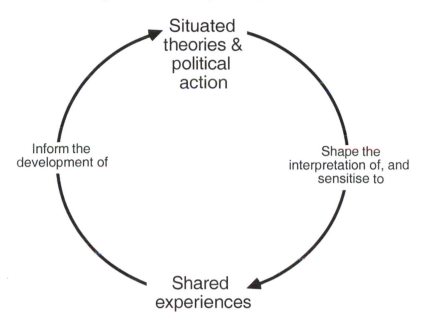

Dorothy Smith (1987), for example, argues that the separation of public and domestic spheres has served to subordinate women through the invisibility of women's subservience to men. Developing out of the women's movement more generally, feminist standpoint methods worked to uncover and undermine the implicit white male standpoint, with its associated political agenda: 'When we assembled as "women" and spoke together as "women", constituting "women" as a category of political mobilization, we discovered dimensions of "our" experience that had no prior discursive definition' (Smith, D. 1997: 394). Theories of women's experience developed by men, standpoint theory argues, silenced and marginalised women, and served the interests of men. An understanding of women's experience from the standpoint of women is better both in the sense that it provides access to the experience of women that would otherwise be invisible and in the sense that it facilitates political resistance to the oppression of women by men.

Feminist standpoint epistemology argues that women have a distinct, and less distorted, way of knowing the world (epistemology) as a consequence of their distinct social position (standpoint) (Harding 1987; Smith, D. 1987). Influenced in part by Marxist epistemology, feminists drew a parallel between the situations, or standpoints, of proletarians (the working class) and women. Harding points out that 'dominant groups have more interests than do those they dominate in not formulating and in excluding questions from how social relations and nature "really work"'(1997: 284). That is to say, while all knowledge is situated, not all standpoints are equally useful ones for understanding social order and inequality. While standpoint theory does not claim that a female standpoint provides the one true account of social reality, it does claim that female standpoints provide a 'less false' (Harding 1987) account of social life. New makes this point clearly: 'Subjugated knowledges can be key to social change, not because they are the whole truth, but because they include information and ways of thinking which dominant groups have a vested interest in suppressing' (1998: 360).

Some critics of standpoint epistemology are concerned that standpoint epistemology leads to relativism. If all knowledge is situated, Hekman argues, the logical consequence of this position is that 'no perspective/standpoint is epistemologically privileged' (1997: 378). However, Dorothy Smith (1997) points out that this argument is really a return to a positivist desire for one true final account. Standpoint theorists reject the dichotomy between absolute truth and relativism. Dorothy Smith (1997) suggests that standpoint epistemology makes the basic sociological move that, if you want to understand society, you need to understand it from the perspective of the people who are participants in it. To understand knowledge as situated and embedded in social relations that are integrally political and practical undermines any pretension to be able to identify one final true account, and also the fear of the bogeyman of relativism. The notion of a standpoint is not individualistic, but refers to a 'historically shared, group-based experience' (Collins 1997: 375). These groups have a degree of stability over time. It is this historical stability, and shared political objectives, that the charge of relativism misunderstands. As Haraway puts it: 'The alternative to relativism is partial, locatable, critical knowledges sustaining the possibility of webs of connections called solidarity in politics and shared conversations in epistemology' (1988: 583).

Feminist standpoint methodology begins with people's experiences. In particular, it focuses on the experiences of women, persons of colour, gays or lesbians, and people who have been excluded from the dominant white male heterosexual standpoint. Standpoint epistemology rejects the idea that there is one true standpoint, highlighting the inherently subjective and political nature of all knowledge. This does not lead to relativism because standpoint methodology focuses on the shared experiences and political concerns of social groups: 'Feminist thought is necessarily concerned with the relationship between social positioning, experience, knowledge, interests and action' (New 1998: 351).

Feminist standpoint epistemology demonstrates that preexisting theory does not only shape what is observed. Preexisting theories are held by people with particular standpoints and political agendas. If women's experience is analysed using only theories and observations from the standpoint of men, the resulting theories oppress women. To analyse women's experience from the standpoint of women both provides 'less false' theories and contributes to the emancipatory task of social justice and equality of the genders. These political dimensions of the interpretive process can no longer be ignored:

> One fundamental feature of this struggle for a self-defined standpoint involves tapping sources of everyday, unarticulated consciousness that have traditionally been denigrated in white, male-controlled institutions (Collins 1990: 26).

Hermeneutics

Simple realism and radical postmodern relativism are both extreme alternatives. Somewhere between these is a recognition that theories are shaped by data, but can never adequately reflect the complex political realities of people's lives. The researcher is never finished exploring, searching, examining and theorising. New depths, complexities, subtleties and uncertainties are continually uncovered. At some point the researcher must stop exploring and write, fixing her or his interpretations in ink with all the inherent political implications. However, human life is fascinating. The researcher trained in exploring and discovering life's complexities will not take long to move beyond what he or she has written. Such is the nature of social research and, at a much more general level, of life: 'The last word for philosophical hermeneutics is not the communication of meaning as such, but the open-endedness of communication in which we continually gain access to the world in which we live' (Risser 1997: 17).

Hermeneutics is the art and science of interpretation. The word 'hermeneutics' derives from the Greek god Hermes, who was a messenger of the gods, interpreting and passing on their messages to humans. In the Christian era hermeneutics was used by theologians to describe the process of biblical interpretation. Hermeneutics is now used much more widely to refer to the art of interpretation generally. In this section I draw primarily on the literature of philosophical hermeneutics (Heidegger 1962; Merleau-Ponty 1962; Gadamer 1975; Ricoeur 1992). I focus on the broad implications of the perspective of philosophical hermeneutics, leaving an examination of the nuances of the varieties of philosophical hermeneutics to more detailed studies (Risser 1997; Kearny 1999). Hermeneutics provides a sophisticated philosophical background for the practice of applied qualitative research (Polkinghorne 1988; Lalli 1989; Crotty 1998).

According to hermeneutics there is no 'truth' behind a performance, nor is there an original version against which a reproduction must be compared. However, this does not mean that there is no truth at all, or that all versions of an experience are the same. Although it involves considerable complexity, 'the Enlightenment was unified by the common belief that reason could transcend contingency to establish universal "truths" and thus guarantee progress' (Tate 1998: 9). Philosophical hermeneutics rejects the enlightenment attempt to find one single transcendental version of the truth. However, it does not fall into extreme relativism either. 'Truth' is bound up with images and performance. This is unavoidable. Hermeneutics engages with the image as a way of discovering truth.

Merleau-Ponty argues that 'the lived life is never entirely comprehensible' and that 'what I understand never quite tallies with my living experience' (1962: 347). This has profound implications, but I will restrict myself to the implications for qualitative data analysis. Merleau-Ponty's analysis means that no interpretation of qualitative data is ever complete. Interpretations are always somewhat uncertain and open-ended. This is disconcerting for people who want to know the 'truth' about this or that issue. Again, it is important to avoid simplistic responses. I am not arguing that all interpretations are the same, or that it does not matter what theory you develop. Data do shape theory, and some theories truthfully represent data and some theories do not. However, 'truth' is not a final and absolute thing. People are not omniscient, or all-knowing. We can never know all the facts. As McGettigan puts it: 'The social world is far too encompassing, evolving, and complex an environment for researchers ever to assume that they have arrived at any of its final truths' (1997: 376). This means that our interpretations are always somewhat provisional, somewhat uncertain, and the facts are always somewhat ambiguous. Humility is required here: a preparedness to listen, to accept that earlier interpretations were inadequate, or could be expanded. However, this humility is combined with fascination—with discovery.

Hermeneutic analysis is like a dance in which the interpretations of the observer and the observed are repeatedly interwoven until a sophisticated understanding is developed: 'Thus the movement of understanding is constantly from the whole to the part and back to the whole . . . The harmony of all the details with the whole is the criterion of correct understanding' (Gadamer 1975: 291). Theory is developed through a continuous movement between preexisting interpretive frameworks, both theoretical and popular, and the data of observation, collected during both intentional observation and everyday life. There is no 'truth' outside this circle. Rather, truth and theory are discovered by engaging with the process of interpretation that is the hermeneutic circle.

Interpretations, and theories, are developed, and continuously redeveloped, within this hermeneutic circle. The role of the hermeneutic circle in the development of theory can be understood in the same way that Ricoeur (1984) understands the role of the hermeneutic circle in the development of narratives. The hermeneutic circle is not a vicious circle. It would be a vicious circle if theory completely shaped what was seen and interpreted. If experiences, or data, are completely unformed and have no structure, then any structure to interpretations—any theory—is completely deceptive. Ricoeur (1984) suggests that this was Nietzsche's argument. However, Ricoeur argues that human experience is structured, and that the hermeneutic circle is a virtuous circle in the sense that the structure of human experience is represented, however uncertain, temporary and limited, by theory and interpretations. Hermeneutics does not try to avoid the hermeneutic circle, nor does it see it as leading to inevitable relativism; rather it engages with the circle of interpretation as a way of understanding human life. As Heidegger put it: 'if we see this circle as a vicious one and look out for ways of avoiding it, even if we just "sense" it as an inevitable imperfection,

Figure 1.7: Hermeneutics

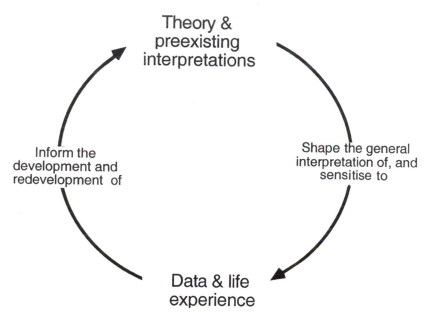

then the act of understanding has been misunderstood from the ground up' (1962: 194).

'Everyday space, then, represents the privileged site of an intersection between what is instituted and what institutes' (Lalli 1989: 110). The material, obdurate nature of experience means that people do not simply invent meanings and interpretations. However, imagination and invention is part of the process through which humans make sense of their world. Following Merleau-Ponty, Polkinghorne suggests that language brings the real to human experience: 'Languages may be the device that allows reality to show forth in experience. Rather than standing in the way of the experience of the real, language may be the lens whose flexibility makes reality appear in sharp focus before experience' (1988: 26). Meaning, Ricoeur argues, is not merely the result of a projection of our understandings onto a meaningless series of events. Rather, the events of lived experience have an 'inchoate narrativity that does not proceed from projecting . . . literature on life, but that constitute a genuine demand for narrativity' (Ricoeur 1984: 74).

Hermeneutics emphasises that the interpretive process is centrally about the tension between one's own perspective and the perspective of the other person: 'Meaning is always negotiated between one's own preconceptions and those within the horizon of the other' (Tate 1998: 13). On the one hand, it is impossible to understand the reality of the other person entirely on his or her own terms. On the other hand, the meanings of the other person are never entirely reduced to our own preconceptions. Thus, interpretation involves an ongoing circular process of moving between one's own perspective and the perspective of the other person: 'The hermeneutic route to understanding is through the iterative use of patterns, metaphors, stories, and models to amplify understanding. We "dialogue" with the phenomenon to be understood, asking what it means to those who create it, and attempt to integrate that with its meaning to us' (Bentz & Shapiro 1998: 111).

> A person who is trying to understand a text is always projecting. He [*sic*.] projects a meaning for the text as a whole as soon as some initial meaning emerges in the text . . . Working out this fore-projection, which is constantly revised in terms of what emerges as he penetrates into the meaning, is understanding what is there (Gadamer 1975: 267).

The interpretive task involves examining 'fore-conceptions' provided by popular understandings and preexisting theory and reworking these interpretations and fore-conceptions 'in terms of the things themselves' (Heidegger 1962: 195): 'The important thing is to be aware of one's own bias, so that the text can present itself in all its otherness and thus assert its own truth against one's own fore-meanings' (Gadamer 1975: 269). Hermeneutics can even be said to have a very modified concept of 'falsifiability': 'An interpretation becomes false whenever the *Sache* [the thing itself] breaks through in conversation to show itself as other than it first presented itself' (Risser 1997: 153). The aim is not to forget previous interpretations, theories or 'fore-conceptions'. Rather, 'all that is asked is that we remain open to the meaning of the other person or text' (Gadamer 1975: 269).

Participating in a tradition is another way of describing the role of preexisting interpretations in the hermeneutic circle. The enlightenment claim to neutral, ahistorical truth ignores the location of all knowledge in a tradition: 'Put in other terms, we are spoken to before we speak; we are posited in tradition before we posit tradition; we are situated before we are free to criticise this situation' (Kearny 1999: 68). Theories are not developed by just thinking and logically reasoning. Rather, as the quote that opens this chapter suggests, it is through an ongoing conversation with other people located in a tradition of conversations that understandings, and theories, are created and recreated (Gadamer 1975: 209). Tradition provides the language and concepts that enable communication to occur. However, tradition is not fixed in the past, nor does it completely determine what is heard and seen. Rather, the hermeneutic circle is an ongoing cycle of interchange between a living, constantly recreated tradition and its interpretation.

Qualitative research draws on a variety of theoretical traditions for the concepts that it utilises, the methods it applies and the modes of communicating its findings. New theories are developed out of, and through, a hermeneutic engagement with these living traditions of knowledge about qualitative research. These traditions neither should be dismissed, nor should they confine completely what is possible. Rather, qualitative research continually builds and rebuilds its practice and theory in response to an engagement with the world, data, experience, or an attempt to hear the voice of the 'other'. A theory, or an interpretive framework, provides a unifying account of events observed in the world, that is temporary, uncertain and limited. Theory is not arrived at solely through logical derivations from abstract principles, nor are theories developed solely through objective observation of an empirical world. Rather, theories are developed through an ongoing dialogue between preexisting understandings and the data, derived from participation in the world.

My own study of illness narratives (Ezzy 2000a) provides an illustration of the hermeneutic approach to theory development. The paper makes use of narrative theory, which is an applied development of hermeneutic theory. I analyse four different theoretical accounts of illness narratives, arguing that these theories misconstrue the temporal aspects of illness narratives. In particular, they all assume that hope can only be understood as controlling the future. I suggest that there may be an alternative form of hope that celebrates life in the present and that does not attempt to control the future. Drawing on qualitative data, the empirical analysis shows that some people living with HIV/AIDS develop a particular illness narrative that constructs a form of hope which celebrates the present. The empirical data analysis provides an elaborated account of hope associated with living in the present. In other words, I draw on an existing theoretical tradition to develop a sensitising theoretical orientation. This sensitising orientation shapes the sorts of questions asked of the data, but does not restrict the data analysis. Through the data analysis the deductively derived theoretical orientation is elaborated, developed, corrected and detailed. This leads on to suggest new theoretical understandings that might be utilised in future research.

Summary reflections

Qualitative research engages with the complexity of analysing human action in terms of meanings. Hermeneutics, postmodernism and symbolic interactionist grounded theory all build theories about how these meanings and interpretations are patterned and produced. Sophisticated practitioners of all three theoretical traditions of qualitative research tend to have developed a similar practice that engages with the cycle of relations between theory and data. However, there are important differences between these theoretical traditions.

Grounded theory originally became popular in the 1960s as a counter-voice to positivist deductive research. Grounded theory still tends to retain traces of an enlightenment understanding of truth, and it is often more acceptable to people who retain an attachment to traditional modernist research practices. This is reflected in denials of the influence of preexisting theory on the research project, the failure to deal adequately with the role of the researcher in the research, and a lack of analysis of the political implications of the research. However, many of these criticisms are no longer true of contemporary symbolic interactionists, who have taken on board many of the insights of the postmodernists.

Postmodernist theory has exposed the failures of enlightenment understandings of truth. K. Daly suggests that, for a postmodernist, 'the challenge for presenting a theoretical text, then, is to present a theory not as objective truth but as a located and limited story, which is fully transparent about who the story teller is and how the teller came to know and present the story' (1997: 360). Postmodernists, such as Derrida, sometimes appear to have slipped into a solipsistic world where language, or text, or theory, is all there is, and the world of action disappears (Kearny 1999). If logically pursued, this leads to a form of theoretical relativism. However, not all postmodernists take this extreme position.

Feminist standpoint epistemologies and methodologies further underlined the failures of an enlightenment understanding of truth, exposing its hidden white masculinist standpoint. In contrast, feminist standpoint epistemologies argue for situated theory that begins with the experience of people from the standpoint studied, and with an emancipatory focus on the politics of change. Standpoint epistemology underlines the essentially political nature of knowledge, and works with the unavoidably situated and historical nature of interpretation.

Hermeneutics provides a sophisticated analysis of the role of theory in data analysis, or the interpretive process. It engages with the effect of preexisting theoretical frameworks on data gathering and analysis, but also recognises the importance of discovery. Hermeneutics aims at being open to understanding the other person. In being open to hear the other person, the researcher aims to listen, to hear some things that might be inconsistent with the researcher's preexisting theory but nonetheless are understood and reinterpreted within theoretical traditions: 'Hermeneutic understanding is, in the end, a matter of communication in which the task of understanding is to find a common language so that the one who speaks can be heard by the other' (Risser 1997: 14).

Postmodernist theory, feminist standpoint epistemology and hermeneutics all lead away from the naive inductivism and simplistic deductivism characteristic of modernist and positivist research. After reading the arguments of these approaches to qualitative research it is no longer possible to pretend that there is one true 'objective' account of 'reality'. Nor is it possible to pretend that politics is irrelevant to theory—but more of that in Chapter 2. I have tried to demonstrate that these new approaches to the role of theory in qualitative research work with the limited, situated nature of theory and data.

Theory produced by qualitative research methods, or any other research method for that matter, does not produce a final account of the nature of reality. Rather, theory is a contribution to an ongoing political dialogue between people with a variety of vested interests. A rigorously conducted qualitative project contributes to this process by providing accounts of people's lives that are less false. The hope is that a better understanding can inform political conversations and political actions, resulting in greater equity and justice.

Theory building mirrors the interpretive processes of everyday life. Theory building is a more systematic process of interpretation. The theorist aims to be more aware of the processes involved, and has a sophisticated tradition of reflection on the process of theory building and data analysis. Qualitative research methods aim to facilitate the discovery of, or the hearing of, the voice of the other, or people, or experience, being studied. It is these qualitative research methods that are examined in the remainder of the book.

Every now and then I notice my New Testament Greek texts and wish I had enough time to practise reading the original Greek. I remember how reading it in Greek made the stories Jesus told come alive. I found this unsettling when I was searching for the one true objective account of the world. I expected systematic treatises, not stories. Although I am not a theologian, it seems to me that Jesus understood that truth was not to be found in systematic accounts that transcend history but in situated contributions to ongoing political conversations. It was Jesus' stories that first drew me to Christianity, and although I am no longer a Christian I have come to a new appreciation of the wisdom of these stories, and stories like them in many other sacred texts. In my search for truth I have arrived back where I started, but with a very different understanding of the nature of truth.

Further reading

Grounded theory

Denzin, N. 1989 *Interpretive Interactionism*, Newbury Park, Sage.
Strauss, A. 1987 *Qualitative Analysis for Social Scientists*, Cambridge, Cambridge University Press.

Postmodernism

Daly, K. 1997 'Re-placing theory ethnography: a postmodern view' *Qualitative Inquiry*, vol. 3, no. 3, pp. 343–66.
Denzin, N. 1997 *Interpretive Ethnography*, Newbury Park, Sage.

Feminist standpoint methodology

Collins, P. 1990 *Black Feminist Thought*, New York, Routledge.
Harding, S. 1986 *The Science Question in Feminism*, New York, Cornell University Press.

——1997 'Comment on Hekman's "truth and method"'
Signs, vol. 22, no. 2, pp. 382–92.

Hermeneutics

Kearny, R. 1999 *Poetics of Modernity: Toward a Hermeneutic
Imagination*, New York, Humanity Books.
Lalli, P. 1989 'The imaginative dimension of everyday life:
towards a hermeneutic reading' *Current sociology*, vol. 37,
no. 1, pp. 103–14.
Polkinghorne, D. 1988 *Narrative Knowing and the Human
Sciences*, Albany, State University of New York Press.

2

Politics, rigour and ethics

Yet both these [quantitative] scientific studies and practitioners' responses share the problem . . . [that] they move from an empirical consideration of rates to a theoretical explanation of *why* the homicide happens without ever considering the homicide event itself. And this is where qualitative sociology offers a unique and constructive approach not only to understanding what is happening in the day-to-day world in which homicide occurs, but to devising policies and programs at the pragmatic levels of city and county government. (Cheatwood 1997: 539)

How is knowledge created? By and for whom? And with what consequences for individuals, groups, and society? (Richardson 1997: 102)

Research always involves politics, and political issues. Research affects social policy, to varying degrees. Research also has political consequences for participants, and this is linked to considerations of rigour and ethics in research practice. In qualitative research, and in qualitative data analysis, these political issues must be addressed to ensure rigorous and relevant research. In this chapter I explore the use of qualitative research methods in the context of applied research: that is, social research designed to answer practical questions with implications for social policy.

Both American pragmatism (which informed symbolic interactionism) and European hermeneutics share a rejection of the ideal of absolute ahistorical truth. However, they both still engage with the world and attempt to make sense of it through developing 'scientific' theory and generalisations: 'The pragmatist and the hermeneut of philosophical hermeneutics do not want to separate reason from the practice of life, and in this sense both are fundamentally Socratic: there is a willingness to talk, to listen to other people, to weigh the consequences of our actions upon other people' (Risser 1997: 115). That is to say, to varying degrees, both theoretical traditions acknowledge the political dimensions of the research process. While feminist methodology has most explicitly incorporated politics in the qualitative research and data analysis, most other theoretical traditions acknowledge also that research is unavoidably political.

This chapter begins with a general discussion of the elements of the policy process, focusing on how qualitative research can provide relevant information. I then review several examples of qualitative research designed to influence the policy process, arguing that for qualitative research to be policy relevant it needs to engage with the worlds and understandings of both policy makers and the participants involved in the research. The second half of the chapter expands this theme, reviewing the contribution of feminism and participatory action research. I demonstrate that qualitative methods can be politically significant for oppressed groups, contributing to a more just and equitable society. Finally, I review different conceptualisations of qualitative rigour, arguing that politics and ethics are central criteria for evaluating the rigour of qualitative research.

Qualitative researchers can no longer ignore the political significance of our research by hiding behind a claim to be objective. Interpreting qualitative data is an inherently political process, and it is better to acknowledge this political dimension at the outset. An explicit engagement with the political and ethical dimensions of qualitative data analysis will result in research that is more insightful, more useful, and more emancipatory in its consequences.

The policy process

There is no clear relationship between social research and policy formulation. Policy makers and practitioners will often use academic studies to support an argument for a particular policy or program. However, if the study conflicts with their political goals they will 'always be able to find methodological reasons to challenge the adequacy of findings' (Travers 1997: 361). This can occur with both quantitative and qualitative research. In quantitative research the use of statistics or particular measures can be questioned. In qualitative research the objection is usually that the research is not representative or reliable. Of all the influences on policy formulation, a balanced assessment of the findings of existing empirical research is just one factor, and often a relatively minor factor at that.

A blatant example of this occurred in the United States in 1998, when President Clinton banned the use of federal funds for needle-exchange programs despite publicly accepting the evidence that these programs are effective strategies for reducing the incidence of HIV (Harris & Goldstein 1998). The American Medical Association, the American Public Health Association, the Surgeon General David Satcher and the head of White House AIDS Policy Sandra Thurman all publicly proclaimed that research has conclusively demonstrated that needle-exchange programs reduce the rate of HIV infection both among injecting drug users and their sexual partners and children, without encouraging drug use. This issue is particularly important in the United States, where half of the new HIV infections are due to the use of intravenous drugs. However, the White House Drug Policy Director, General Barry McCaffrey, claimed to have changed the President's mind when he argued that 'studies supporting needle-exchanges were incomplete and that more research on the matter is required' (Bedard 1998: 1). The refusal to allow the use of federal funds for needle exchanges was more likely a product of pressure from the Republican-dominated Congress, which would have overturned the decision if Clinton had allowed the use of federal funds. In other words, social research plays only a secondary role in much social policy formulation.

We should not conclude from this one example that research is irrelevant to the policy process. Although the decision went against the actions suggested by research, the social policy debate about funding needle-exchanges had to both engage with and respond to the established body of research. In contrast, and consistent with the social policy implications of research, Australia has had needle-exchange programs for some time. The debate in Australia has more recently turned to the funding of safe injecting rooms. This also has been linked to reducing the incidence and spread of HIV/AIDS. Social research, and more particularly qualitative research, can have an important effect on policy making. However, first we need a more sophisticated understanding of social policy.

Social policy is a process. Social policy is not formulated as part of a single decision-making event (Weiss 1982). Decision makers do not typically sit around a room reviewing the research findings, considering alternative possibilities of action, and then deciding on a chosen program. Decision making is often a long process, involving reversals and pauses and transformations. Decision makers often do not meet as a group, and factors that influence one decision maker may be irrelevant to another. Rist argues that 'the reorientation away from "event decision making" and to "process decision making" necessitates looking at research as serving an "enlightenment function" in contrast to an "engineering function"' (1994: 546).

The 'engineering perspective' argues that social research can provide detailed knowledge about particular social problems that can be then used to engineer particular desired outcomes. However, as a consequence of the complex and continually changing nature of social life, research findings rarely provide enough data or detail to allow the specifics of a particular policy to be evaluated, or outcomes assured. Social research is rarely detailed enough to perform an 'engineering function' in policy decision making. Rather, social research serves a broader function by providing general 'enlightenment' about the contexts, structures and nuances of a particular issue. If policy makers are well educated about the general nature of an issue, so the enlightenment argument goes, then they will be better equipped to assess particular policy initiatives. For example, the more exposure policy makers have to research about the experience and nature of illicit drug use in contemporary society, the more likely they are to develop policies that will produce socially desirable outcomes.

Qualitative research can aim to provide information that will perform this 'enlightenment function' for policy makers and their advisers. Rigorous, well-researched qualitative reports have informed Australian policy on a variety of issues, such as unemployment (Windschuttle 1979; Brewer 1980), anorexia (Garrett 1998) and HIV prevention (McLeod & Nott 1994). There are, of course, many other studies. This research provides a better understanding of the processes operating in these areas and supports a more informed social policy, although there will always be many factors other than social research that influence social policy.

The social policy process can be thought of as a cycle with three stages: policy formulation, policy implementation and policy evaluation (Guba 1984; Rist 1994). Different information is required at each stage of the policy cycle. Policy researchers, and qualitative researchers in particular, should be aware of the particular stage of the policy process their research is aimed at and the distinctive needs and logic of that stage.

Policy-relevant information that can be provided by qualitative research

• Policy formulation
 — Define the problem.
 — Describe previous policy responses.
 — Evaluate the relevance of previous policies to the current problem.
• Policy implementation
 — Evaluate the policy implementation process: are goals being achieved?
 — Monitor the problem: is it changing?
 — How are organisations and communities responding to the problem?
• Policy evaluation
 — How has the policy changed community understandings of the problem?
 — Monitor the problem: is it changing?
 — Evaluate the organisational dynamics of policy implementation.
(Rist 1994)

Policy formulation involves defining the problem, reviewing previous responses to the problem, and evaluating current options. Policy formulation therefore includes three main clusters of questions or information needs (Rist 1994). First, policy makers must define the problem, map its dimensions and specify the particular conditions under which it is most common. Second, previous policy responses to the problem need to be described, evaluated and detailed. Third, information is required about how previous experiences can be used to inform choices between policies in the present. If needle-exchange programs were rejected ten years ago, why were they rejected, and are there different factors operating at the present time? Qualitative research can be very relevant to this stage of policy formulation. The work of defining the problem and reviewing previous work often occurs as part of a qualitative study. Unfortunately, qualitative research that focuses on this aspect of policy is rarely funded, as policy makers usually have a short time available between when a problem is identified and the need for a formulated response to this problem. However, it does point to the need for a well-funded level of basic research that, while not directly relevant to current policy priorities, may become relevant as priorities change over time.

Policy implementation involves translating policies into programs of action: 'The concern becomes one of how to use the available resources in the most efficient and effective manner in order to have the most robust impact on the program or condition at hand' (Rist 1994: 550). Again there are three main clusters of questions or information needs. First, the process of policy implementation itself requires evaluating in terms of whether it is achieving its goals and providing resources among the target communities or audiences. Qualitative methods provide an excellent way of obtaining information about the day-to-day implementation of programs. Second, the problem that the policy was designed to respond to requires ongoing monitoring. Are conditions improving, remaining the same, or is some other factor changing the nature of the problem? Third, the understandings and responses of various organisations and communities with an interest in the issue need to be monitored. Clearly qualitative research provides an excellent way of assessing how relevant workers and decision makers are reacting to the policy and its implementation.

Policy evaluation takes place later in the policy cycle. The issue here is whether program objectives have been achieved. First, qualitative research methods can examine the changes in understandings and interpretations that may have resulted from a particular program in a depth not available to other research methods. This information can be important in assessing the effectiveness of future policies. Second, as with research at the policy implementation stage, qualitative research can be used to monitor changes in the condition or problem. Third, qualitative methods are particularly useful in describing the organisational workings of particular programs that may have affected outcomes. Staff turnover or organisational problems may influence a program's effectiveness, and 'these are true qualitative dimensions of organizational life' (Rist 1994: 553).

Examples of applied qualitative research

This section reviews four qualitative studies that have influenced, or hope to influence, social policy: Shiner and Newburn's (1997) study of drug use among young people; Bourdieu's (1993) study of poverty in France; Travers' (1997) review of two studies of criminal justice; and Church and Creal's (1995) research with psychiatric survivors. Each study deals with a different aspect of the role of qualitative research in social policy formulation, implementation and evaluation.

Michael Shiner and Tim Newburn describe the importance of qualitative research for an understanding of the changing attitudes of young people to drug use in the United Kingdom. A simplistic interpretation of survey data has led some researchers to suggest that drug use has become normal among young people—an idea that they call the 'normalisation thesis'. The normalisation thesis appears to be designed to generate outrage among adults at the drug use of young people. Shiner and Newburn criticise the normalisation thesis from two perspectives. First, surveys have shown that surprisingly large numbers of young people report drug use. For example, one study found that one-third of young people between the ages of 14 and 21 reported ever having used a drug (Shiner & Newburn 1997: 514). However, there is an enormous difference between those *ever* having used a drug and those who are current users. Nearly half of the people who said that they had ever used a drug said that they had not done so in the past year. Second, there is a significant difference in the understandings of different types of drugs, with cannabis, party drugs and hard drugs showing different patterns of use. The advocates of the normalisation thesis appear to be confusing the one-off use of a drug with the idea that drug use has become normal and accepted behaviour among young people.

Drawing on a qualitative study, Shiner and Newburn first demonstrate that among both non-drug users and drug users there are very different understandings of cannabis and other drugs. While cannabis use may be becoming more accepted, this does not translate into the general acceptance of all 'illegal substances'. Party drugs, for example, are limited to a relatively small minority, and 'hard drugs' such as cocaine and heroin are rarely used. Second, they demonstrate that even among people who have used drugs there is an acceptance of the view that drug use is not a normal behaviour. Rather it is seen as a deviant behaviour, and drug users employ neutralisation techniques to justify their own drug use. That is to say, the meaning current drug users give to their behaviour is not the same as the meaning of drug use that proponents of the normalisation thesis had assumed.

In other words, the argument that drug use has become normal among young people is a significant misunderstanding of young people's practice and interpretation of drug use. To have once used a drug does not imply that drug use is accepted as normal. To have used, or to be currently using, cannabis does not imply that all drugs are accepted as normal. Finally, even those young people currently using drugs do not necessarily see drug use as a normal part of their life. If drug use had indeed become normalised among young people this would have very different policy implications from where drug use remained a behaviour rarely practised and typically understood as deviant by the majority of young people.

How useful is this sort of qualitative research? The project described provides background information that presumably the authors hope will serve a general 'enlightenment' function, by better informing policy makers' understandings of drug use. However, there are a number of reasons for suspecting that this research may not have the sort of influence desired by its authors.

All academic researchers would like their research to have the sort of influence that Pierre Bourdieu's (1993, English edn 1999) work, *The Weight of the World: Social Suffering in Contemporary Society*, has had in France. His research aims to make publicly visible forms of social inequality and poverty that are hidden by traditional measures and indicators. Wacquant reports that the book 'sold over 100,000 copies in three months and stood atop the best-seller list for months; it was extensively discussed in political circles and popular magazines alike (conservative Prime Minister Balladur publicly ordered his cabinet members to read it)' (1998: 322). It is rare for social research to be as influential as Bourdieu's work. Academic research is seldom as influential on the policy process as researchers would wish, and this is likely to be the fate of Shiner and Newburn's (1997) research. Max Travers' (1997) discussion of the influence, or lack of influence, of criminal justice research applies more generally. He argues that the low profile of much research is not simply a product of different political persuasions. It is not that predominantly liberal or left-wing research is out of step with an increasingly right-wing society.

Rather, he argues that the irrelevance of the research is a product of the way it is conducted and written. Research is conducted in particular ways, written in such a style and published in particular journals, that together result in its being heard only by people who share similar understandings of the issues discussed.

Travers (1997) reviews two qualitative studies of criminal justice in the United Kingdom that criticise the criminal justice system. One study (McConville et al. 1991) argues that police have too much discretionary power and make arbitrary decisions. The other (McConville 1994) demonstrates the failings and inadequacies of criminal defence solicitors. Both claim to be objective studies of an empirical social problem. Travers observes that the focus of the empirical material, including the selection of supporting quotes and illustrations, is clearly set up to make the point that the current criminal justice system is unjust. This means that it is relatively easy for someone with a differing understanding of the criminal justice system to dismiss the findings as biased. For example, it would be relatively easy to imagine a different set of researchers selecting a different set of quotes and illustrations to support the contention that the police and criminal lawyers are doing the best they can in difficult times. However, the most telling comment is Travers' conclusion that: 'One suspects that many criminal lawyers will have difficulty in recognizing their day-to-day activities in this text, and this will weaken its persuasiveness in raising the issue of quality in relation to defence work' (1997: 371).

If qualitative research is to be heard by relevant groups and people, then it must engage with the understandings and assumptions of these groups and people as audiences of the text. Travers, for example, points out that neither of the texts he reviews make a sophisticated attempt to represent what the symbolic interactionists have called 'the actor's point of view': 'To some extent this results from the methodological basis of these studies which seek to make a general case by presenting decontextualized examples of practices they disagree with, rather than attempting to explicate or address how the police or defence lawyers understand the particular people and situations they encounter in the course of their day-to-day activities' (1997: 373). Travers argues that 'thicker' descriptions (Geertz 1973) should be provided of the activities under study that include an attempt to explain how the practitioners understand their activities. This allows the practitioners to recognise themselves in the report and encourages them to take it seriously as an 'objective' document. As a consequence the report is more likely to be taken up and read as part of a debate that may develop and change professional practice. The aim of 'objectivity' in this sense is not that of scientifically accurate description. Rather, 'objectivity' is a socially generated assessment of the text that indicates that it is recognised by participants and relevant groups as dealing with their understandings and experiences of the issues and problems examined. A good example of the sort of engaged research Travers advocates is Church's research with psychiatric survivors.

Kathryn Church and Liz Creal's (1995) *Voices of Experience* is a report on a qualitative study of the implementation of various community businesses, including two run by psychiatric survivors. The report describes the ongoing work of non-profit businesses that are owned by the community or the workers, operate with participatory management, and have the target of hiring the long-term unemployed: 'The response to the "Voices of Experience" was tremendous from a variety of groups: study participants; workers in frontline health, social service and anti-poverty agencies; academics in universities' (Church 1997: 3). In particular, mental health policy makers and planners were impressed with the idea and practice of businesses run by psychiatric survivors. The effect of this qualitative research was to facilitate further funding from a government agency to allow the ongoing work of community economic development among psychiatric survivors to continue. In other words, this qualitative research played a major role in providing information about the success of the implementation of a particular policy, and this information in turn shaped future policy and practice.

Church (1995) makes the point that the priorities of her research were not developed in the usual academic way. In most research, the goals and objectives of the research are developed out of a review of academic literature. Most research is driven by theoretical aims. However, for Church, her research was motivated and shaped by her experiences as an activist for psychiatric survivors. Her research was informed by political activities and strategies of the various mental health and psychiatric survivor organisations in which she was involved. Reviewing the academic literature came after Church had already spent considerable time working in and with organisations and individuals involved in her area of study: 'In order to produce an accessible knowledge of "consumer participation", I began with action rather than academic literature' (Church 1995: 15). She tried to begin planning her research project by discussing it with Pat, a leader of the psychiatric survivor community. She wrote a memo outlining her ideas, and arranged a meeting:

> Instead of engaging with my project, Pat suggested a different course of action. I needed to get myself 'roughed up' on the front line, see what the lives of the people were really like. She suggested I go down and see how things were at Parkdale Activity and Recreation Centre . . . I agreed. Pat met me at PARC, introduced me to the regulars, showed me around the building. I spent the afternoon chopping onions for the evening meal and trying to talk with people whose worlds were a mystery to me. Pat was at home, confident and competent; I was an outsider, uncertain and awkward (Church 1995: 26).

If qualitative research is to assess and inform policy and practice, then it must also be informed by the practicalities and priorities of the organisations and people involved. It is the tension between theoretical academic aims and practical organisational objectives that Church brings to our attention. This tension is not resolved simply by discussing the formulation of the aims with policy makers and practitioners. Rather, the design and conduct of the research is intimately related to applied issues and problems.

Feminism and participatory action research

> In order to understand a thing, one must change it (Mies 1991: 63).

Political and methodological concerns raised by feminists and participatory action researchers have a more general significance for the practice of qualitative research. This section reviews both feminist insights and participatory action research with a view to examining how the insights of these two traditions can be applied to qualitative research. I examine feminist advocacy for the value of qualitative methods, and then review the role of emancipatory politics in social research. I argue that the political dimensions of social research must be explicitly addressed in all qualitative research.

Feminist methodology, as the name suggests, emphasises the primary nature of gender as a category of experience, arguing that it should therefore be primary in data analysis. Mainstream social science routinely silences and masks women and women's concerns. For example, research on the sociology of work typically ignores issues such as emotional labour and domestic work in favour of the public masculine world of paid employment (Elshtain 1981). Dorothy Smith argues that feminist research attempts to redress the imbalance in existing research: 'Until recently, established sociology had a concealed gender subtext . . . it was thought, investigated, and written largely from the perspective of men' (1987: 152). There is no single 'feminist methodology'. Feminists use both qualitative and quantitative methods and a variety of methods within each of these genres. Reinharz (1992) argues that rather than trying to provide a single list that defines feminist methodology, it is more useful to recognise the variety of feminist methodologies, with the emphasis on the plural, that are all involved in an ongoing discussion about the nature of knowledge.

Participatory action research combines participatory and action research. It aims to provide an integrated process in which research, education and action all draw on the skills of all participants (researcher and researched), with the goal of increasing the knowledge of all participants and enabling social transformation (Brydon-Miller 1997). Nelson and associates describe the value of combining participatory and action research: 'From participatory research we recognize power imbalances and the need to engage oppressed people as agents of their own change. From action research, we recognize the value of engaging other stakeholders and of using research findings to inform intervention decisions' (1998: 885). Participatory action research has been utilised in a number of contexts, including research in developing countries, and often focused on issues and problems for oppressed minorities (Rice & Ezzy 1999).

This section discusses feminist research and participatory action research together because I am primarily interested in their implications for the practice of social research in general, rather than in examining and describing the detail of each of these particular research traditions. Both feminism and participatory action research have demonstrated that qualitative research is unavoidably political and personal.

The value of qualitative methods

The feminist critique of social science research methodology argues that objectivity, and quantitative methodology, is often an ideological screen for masculine interests: 'The supposedly objective sciences are blind to women's issues' (Mies 1991: 60). Women's voices were rarely heard when surveys and statistics were deployed. Feminists pointed to how quantitative research techniques were often biased because they included only male subjects, and then followed this sampling bias with inaccurate interpretation, through assuming that a theory tested on men held also for women (Jayaratne & Stewart 1991).

In response to the clear bias of quantitative research methods, feminists argued for the value of qualitative methods: 'Accordingly, the early feminist methodology texts all celebrated qualitative methods as best suited to the project of hearing women's accounts of their experiences' (Oakley 1998: 708). The emphasis on women's personal testimonies, often linked to a consciousness-raising agenda, resulted in a preference for qualitative methods. In the attempt to make audible women's voices, to make visible their concerns and understandings, many feminists have utilised qualitative methods, particularly those that encouraged women's testimony.

In a context where women's voices have been systematically ignored by researchers both in theory and method, qualitative methods, particularly long interviews, are important because they offer 'researchers access to people's ideas, thoughts, and memories in their own words rather than in the words of the researcher' (Reinharz 1992: 19). This echoes the point made by the grounded theorists that research framed by preexisting theory constrains and forces data collection and analysis. Feminist theorists utilise qualitative methods to hear the voices of women masked by quantitative methods.

More generally, it could be argued that qualitative methods are more likely to represent the interests of underdogs and outsiders (Becker & Horowitz 1972; Lincoln 1995). Through the attempt to be closer to the lived experience of the people being studied, qualitative methods are less likely to make unwarranted assumptions about the meaning and significance of experience for women, or any other research subjects for that matter. Qualitative methods explicitly identify a person's understanding of the situation as something to be discovered rather than assumed. This is particularly important for groups whose experiences and understandings have been oppressed and repressed by dominant policies and research methods—although, as Gouldner (1975) noted in his incisive analysis of Howard Becker's ethnographic interactionism, such a perspective does not prevent the research findings also being consistent with the interests of one or another politically powerful group.

Feminists have subsequently argued that the problem is not with the methodology of quantitative research, as such, but with how it is done, and the uses to which it is put. It is quite possible to use quantitative methods to further the political interests of women. Jayaratne and Stewart, for example, quote a quantitative study that exposed very high maternal death rates among black women in Chicago. The study was used to argue for increased funding for this group of women: 'The greatest benefit of apparent objectivity lies in its power to change political opinion' (1991: 100). That is to say, by the feminist criteria of improving women's status, quantitative research methods may be very useful. Oakley (1998) takes this a step further when she draws on object relations theory to argue that the division between quantitative and qualitative methods reinforced by feminist theory may have the unintended consequence of continuing to construct women as the 'other' against which some may discriminate: 'The feminist case against quantification is ultimately unhelpful to the goal of an emancipatory social science' (Oakley 1998: 708).

Early feminist researchers were vocal advocates of qualitative research methods. The value of qualitative methods for feminists is that qualitative methods allow women's voices to be heard when existing theory, and research based on this theory, systematically suppresses women's voices. Qualitative methods are better equipped to discover the voice of the 'other' than are quantitative methods. However, once women's voices had begun to be articulated, many feminists argued that surveys and other quantitative methods could usefully serve the feminist goal of emancipatory politics. The next section examines the explicit incorporation of political issues in research methodology.

The unavoidably political consequences of research

Feminist and participatory action research demonstrates that research inevitably has political consequences. Further, feminism and participatory action research argue that political consequences are the responsibility of the researcher. For example, Lather argues that researchers should be concerned not only about the quality of their data but also with the political consequences of their research, with 'praxis': 'What I suggest is that we consciously use our research to help participants understand and change their situations' (Lather 1991: 57).

It is the focus on change for women that makes research distinctively feminist. Mies puts this point provocatively when she argues that 'the aim of the women's movement is not just the study but the overcoming of women's oppression and exploitation' (1991: 62). Feminist methodology is committed to a political response to gender inequality. Reflecting the consciousness-raising focus of the broader feminist movement, feminist research methodology is centrally concerned with 'various efforts to include women's lives and concerns in accounts of society, to minimize the harms of research, and to support changes that will improve women's status' (De Vault 1996: 29).

Feminists have varied considerably in the way that they understand the contribution of their research to emancipatory politics. Coates, Dodds and Jensen define 'feminist action-oriented research as research that is designed to allow people both to understand and to change inequitable distributions of power, knowledge, and resources with the intention of contributing to anti-oppression movements' (1998: 332). Other researchers have utilised the concept of 'praxis' to refer to the integration of empirical research and political action in feminist methodology. Stanley defines feminist praxis as 'a political position in which "knowledge" is not simply defined as "knowledge *what*" but also as "knowledge *for*". Succinctly, the point is to change the world, not only to study it' (1990: 13, original emphasis). More generally, some feminist research is linked to communitarian ethics that entail a commitment to particular forms of social organisation as being more just (Benhabib 1992; Denzin 1997).

Action researchers have similarly argued that the best way to learn about social issues is to try to change them (Lewin 1946). Lewin proposed a cyclical process involving problem definition, the finding of information, identifying goals, implementing action, and simultaneously evaluating these actions, leading into a new cycle of problem solving. Action research has often been associated with organisational change and managerial practice, and tended to be less concerned about the power differences and emancipatory social change that have motivated feminists and participatory research.

The classic distinction between personal troubles and public issues, first described by Mills (1959), is also deployed by participatory action research and feminists. Dickson puts this clearly when she describes a commitment to educating participants, particularly in the sociopolitical analysis of problems being studied that involves 'shifting the interpretation of problems from an individual to a societal context and an ecological relationship' (2000: 189).

Feminists point to the exploitative nature of the traditional research relationship, where the researcher receives all the rewards, and research findings are not reported in a manner useful to research participants (Jayaratne & Stewart 1991). In other words, traditional research has been supportive politically of the status quo, while hiding behind a veil of methodological neutrality. Research is always political. To pretend that research is not political is to be supportive of current structures and practices without saying so explicitly. This has led feminists to argue for the need to integrate political goals, designed to benefit women, as an integral part of the research process.

Knowledge is not monopolised by professionals but is decentralised, and its associated power should be distributed to participants in research. In most research, subjects are treated more like objects 'to be studied, known, and acted on, ostensibly for their own ultimate good and the benefit of others' (Dickson 2000: 189). In participatory action research, people are not acted on, but are treated as genuine subjects, with their own thoughts, ideas and assessments. They participate fully in the research process, often with a considerable degree of control over the goal and method of the research (Hall, S. 1981).

An excellent example of participatory action research is provided by Dickson (2000), who conducted research with a group of Canadian Aboriginal grandmothers. Dickson describes a project involving fourteen Aboriginal grandmother participants meeting weekly for formal learning, organising and informal support over a two-and-a-half-year period. The participants developed greater self-understanding, strategies for individual health maintenance, learned information about health issues and resources, began to identify with the group and became politically engaged through a desire to influence the broader social system, through public speaking and community recognition. The combination of personal empowerment and sociopolitical activity was one of the reasons for the success of the project. In conclusion, Dickson argues that 'this article shows changes toward empowerment and health that are possible through the intervention of participatory action research and health promotion programming with individuals who are multiply disadvantaged, undeserved, and at risk of premature ill health. The findings argue for respectful, sustained, and culturally appropriate supports to foster personal and community resiliency, restore traditional roles and responsibilities, and allay early disease and death' (2000: 211).

Silenced voices.

But did you ever think to speak up?
Sometimes at home
I would want to
disagree with my husband
but I didn't.
Sometimes in town
I would want to
speak up on something
but I didn't.
Now
We're old but we're many.
Now
We're asked and they listen.
Now
We're speaking up like we should.
(Dickson 2000: 210)

To be supportive of—even celebrate—the status quo is often an important political statement. While inequality needs to be redressed, there is much of social life that is wonderful as it is and deserves to be celebrated. A good example of this is Gary Alan Fine's (1998) work on the culture of mushrooming! While there are political dimensions, for example linked to debates about the environment, this is a classic qualitative symbolic interactionist study that explores a seemingly unusual activity to describe basic social processes. Fine tells his story with a sense of humour and appreciation of the pleasures of mushroom collecting. Simply, qualitative research is political, but not everything needs changing.

Politics is integral to research. From the perspective of hermeneutics, Charles Taylor (1989) has argued that it is impossible to describe an identity without also, simultaneously, evaluating that identity. A story about oneself, or any story for that matter, is simultaneously a description and an evaluation. While some qualitative research may appear to be less politically contentious than other research, the political consequences of a research project are an important consideration that can no longer be ignored or taken for granted by researchers. It is no longer possible to hide behind the claim to be 'just describing what is happening'. The onus is now on the qualitative researcher to take seriously the political consequences of his or her research.

Rigour and ethics

A number of years ago now I was sitting in a small one-bedroom flat not far from Oxford Street in Sydney, in the heart of the gay and HIV ghetto. I had been talking to a gay man with HIV, diagnosed some eight years prior to our meeting. A number of his close friends had died of AIDS. He began telling me about his life, his part-time work, his periods of unemployment, his exercise regimen, and his sex life. A discussion of sex was not uncommon among my interviewees. Sex is, after all, the issue at the heart of living with HIV if you are a sexually promiscuous gay man. However, this man was different. He openly confided in me that he regularly had casual sex at particular venues without using a condom and without discussing his HIV status with his sexual partners. The man looked healthy and he told me his viral load (an indicator of disease progression) was low. He seemed to want me either to reprimand him or to publicise the information he was providing to scare off his sexual partners.

During the weeks after that interview I worried about what I should do. Do I report him? Do I present a transcript of my tape to a gay newspaper so that others could be warned? Should I contact him and reprimand him? What was the ethically and politically astute action to take? Eventually I rang a friend involved in HIV and gay politics. He reminded me that we already knew this sort of thing was happening. It showed up in a variety of surveys of gay men's sexual practice. If I took it to the papers it would just create hysteria that would only damage the trust and openness that was the foundation of Australia's safe-sex culture and the reason why so few people in Australia had HIV. The most appropriate response would be to inform the relevant workers at the local AIDS Council. Creating a media moral panic about unsafe sex would not help prevent unsafe sex. It would make people even more unwilling to disclose their status. Local workers were best placed to talk to the relevant people and perhaps to place targeted safe-sex messages. This is, of course, a variation on the peer debriefing described in Chapter 3.

Ethical conduct of qualitative research is much more than following guidelines provided by ethics committees. It involves a weighed consideration of both how data collection is conducted and how analysed data are presented, and will vary significantly depending on the details and particularities of the situation of the research. Similarly, criteria for assessing whether qualitative research is rigorous cannot simply be assessed by whether the research followed particular objective criteria. Rigour in qualitative research is as much situated and linked to the politics and particularities of the research as it is to following established methods and practices.

In the following discussion I review three sets of criteria for assessing rigour in qualitative research. I also discuss the associated understandings of ethical research that are linked to each model of rigour. Rigour and ethics were originally considered to be quite separate. Rigour deals with correct method, and ethics deals with correct moral conduct. However, under the influence of postmodernist, feminist and hermeneutic theory, it has become increasingly clear that all knowledge is inextricably moral with ethical implications. Descriptions of rigour in qualitative research have therefore increasingly included ethical conduct as part of the criteria for rigorous research, rather than as external to it.

The first model draws on the methods and criteria of natural science. Although this model is now largely discredited among many qualitative researchers, it retains considerable influence because of its consistency with the natural science models of research that remain influential in the more general research community (e.g. Mays & Pope 1995). The natural science model of rigour in qualitative research accepts the aim of objectivity and the logic of the scientific paradigm (see text box, p.52). It seeks to provide a set of criteria parallel to the criteria the natural sciences use for establishing rigour. This model of rigour emphasises terms such as validity, reliability and objectivity as central methodological criteria. It assumes that rigorous research findings accurately reflect an external objective world. This can be described as involving a 'foundationalist episte-mology' because knowledge is thought to rest on the foundation of an objective external world (Lincoln 1995). Validity refers to whether a scientific theory is internally coherent, and to whether it accurately reflects this external world. Reliability refers to the ability to repeat the research and find the same results. Objective research, according to this model, is research that has been uninfluenced by the values, interests and hopes of the researcher, which are subjective and not scientific. When this natural sciences model is applied to qualitative research, the typical result is a mixture of natural science and inter-pretive criteria.

Natural science model of rigour in qualitative research

- Theory—The development of substantive and formal theory (internal validity).
- Novelty—Research should provide new insights.
- Empirical consistency—Theoretical claims should be demon-strably consistent with empirical observations (external validity).
- Credibility—Readers and participants should find the account credible (objectivity).
- Transferability—Findings should be transferable to other settings (reliability).
- Reflexivity—The effect of the research method on the results should be clear (objectivity).
  (Adapted from Athens 1984; Lincoln & Guba 1985; Hammersley 1998.)

Linked to this natural sciences model of rigour is a natural sciences model of what constitutes ethics. It assumes that the ethical nature of research can be guaranteed through the review of methods by ethics committees and following the procedures of informed consent. While these are useful safeguards against ethical misconduct, they do not ensure the ethical conduct of researchers in the field.

The standard of informed consent that is required by most ethics committees assumes a natural sciences model of the conduct of research in which the researcher is an expert and remains aloof from the participants of the study (Emerson 1983). Further, it assumes that research is conducted with individuals in clearly defined research encounters, almost like a laboratory experiment (Thorne 1980). This is clearly problematic for researchers who use methods such as participant observation or ethnography. It is also problematic for researchers whose theory is informed by interactionist, feminist or postmodernist insights that research evolves through an ongoing relationship between the researcher and the researched. In these cases researchers may also be part of the participants' community, or may live with participants for a period of time.

There are other major problems in applying this natural sciences model to the practices of qualitative research. Qualitative researchers are typically concerned with the meanings and interpretations that people give to their experiences. These meanings and interpretations constantly change in response to the changing conditions of contemporary social life. It may, therefore, be impossible to replicate a research project as is required by reliability. Goffman's (1961) research on mental illness cannot be replicated, for example, because mental hospitals and mental illness are now treated and organised very differently. Further, events do not have one clear meaning; rather, they are polyvalent. Part of the attraction of some television programs, for example, is that they are intentionally designed and written so that they can be interpreted in many different ways by a variety of social groups. Qualitative researchers are not immune from this process. The idea that a theory should accurately reflect the experiences of social life (validity) is clearly problematic if there is not one clear meaning of a social experience. This does not mean that all interpretations are equally correct. Some theories are clearly better explanations than others. However, the criteria for whether a theory is a better explanation cannot simply be whether it validly reflects the experience being studied. Finally, contemporary theorists have demonstrated that subjective interpretations always influence the process of knowing and understanding that is at the foundation of qualitative research (Game 1991; Denzin 1997). To try to be 'objective' is therefore to pretend that our preconceptions and biases are not influencing our research when they actually are an unavoidable influence on research practice. It is better to acknowledge how our subjective preconceptions and biases shape the research, and to deal with these biases openly and honestly, rather than to pretend they do not exist.

It is relatively easy to deconstruct the natural sciences model of qualitative research by demonstrating the problems associated with applying natural sciences methods to the social world. It is much harder to construct an alternative. If the old model does not make sense any more, what can be used instead as criteria for assessing the rigour, quality and trustworthiness of qualitative research?

Contemporary models of rigour in qualitative research tend to be of two types. First there are those that focus on the interpretive process (see text box below). These models emphasise obtaining high- quality description through a sensitivity to the complexity of the meanings, feelings and interpretations of participants and researchers. This model tends to reject the correspondence model of truth that emphasises the role of validity and reliability. In qualitative research, 'the key problem is understanding how individuals interpret events and experiences, rather than assessing whether or not their interpretations correspond to or mirror the researchers' interpretive construct of "objective" reality' (Mishler 1990: 427).

Some researchers still argue that the quality of description and interpretation are central to what constitutes rigorous qualitative research. Gubrium and Holstein (1997), for example, suggest a set of criteria that they describe as the 'new language of qualitative method'. Their approach deserves careful consideration, and the issues they raise are an important part of what constitutes rigorous qualitative research (see text box below). While they have removed many of the hangovers of the natural sciences model, they do not deal with the integrally political nature of qualitative research.

Interpretive model of rigour in qualitative research

- Scepticism—Qualitative research is sceptical of the quality of common sense and quantitative understandings of social life.
- Close scrutiny—Research involves getting 'close' to the world of the people being studied and noticing the detail of their experiences and interpretations.
- Thick description—Research should provide a rich, clear and nuanced description of social life.
- Focus on process—Social life is continuously actively constructed as part of a process that constructs and transforms social life.
- Appreciation of subjectivity—Social life is integrally subjective, made up of meanings, interpretations and feelings, and it cannot be understood without examining this subjective experience.
- Tolerance for complexity—Simple explanations are not typically the best. Social life and contemporary culture are a complex web of significations and interpretations that shape human action. Research needs to appreciate and address this complexity.

(Summarised from Gubrium & Holstein 1997.)

The emphasis on interpretive understanding suggests an ethical approach that also relies on the understandings of participants. Irvine (1999: 182) argues that 'if one wants to understand what takes place within group settings, it is essential to understand—and respect—the ethical standards of the group'. In her research with a Codependents Anonymous group, she reports that she did not conform to the required standards of informed consent as defined by her institutional ethics committee. To have done so would have violated the norms of the groups she was studying. Rather, through listening and participating, she developed a research methodology that respected the standard practice of the group she was studying. Irvine argues that this practice represents a more egalitarian understanding of the respective statuses of researcher and participant.

A more provocative approach to rigour is taken by researchers strongly influenced by postmodernist and hermeneutic theory (Clough 1992; Lather 1993; Denzin 1997). They argue for the integrally political nature of social research (see text box, p. 56). Rejecting the distinction between facts and values, these researchers maintain that rigorous methods must integrate research and political action (Lincoln 1995). The political model of rigour is typically influenced by the work of the feminists and participant action researches described in Chapter 1.

Ethical research from this perspective is integrally linked to a commitment to political action and participant inclusion. The issues discussed in Chapter 3, such as the inclusion and co-option of participants' voices, become issues not just of political orientation but also of ethics (Herndl & Nahrwold 2000).

'First, do no harm' (Hippocratic oath). This applies as much to activities during data collection as it does to report writing and choices made during data analysis. It applies, for example, to decisions about whether to report practices that may be considered secret, or that may discredit subjects: 'A field researcher discovers many reprehensible activities, but they lack warrant for disclosing them. What does one do when one is compelled to write critically about one's informants, who may well be one's friends? It could be justifiable, possibly even compulsory, but on what basis is this to be decided?' (Liberman 1999: 62). I began this section by describing an ethical dilemma of precisely this form. My response was not a product of following guidelines, nor was it just the result of talking to others working in the same field. My response also grew out of a desire to do what was best, as I understood it, for the community, and specifically for people living with HIV/AIDS.

According to a number of contemporary commentators, at the heart of an ethical commitment to justice must also be a genuine respect for the 'other' (Taylor 1992; Bauman 1998). This point applies equally well to the practices of qualitative research. As Liberman observes: 'On many occasions a great portion of the ethics of our sociological practice derives from having a genuine, and not merely feigned, respect for the social practices that we study' (1999: 55). Drawing on the language of hermeneutic theory discussed in Chapter 1, qualitative research aims both to hear the voice of the other and to respect the rights of the other. Respect for the other, and hence the ethical conduct of the researcher towards the participant, is integrally bound up with a practice that attempts to listen carefully to the experience and voice of the other (Taylor 1992; Bauman 1998).

Ethics in fieldwork is difficult to formalise. There are a number of reasons for this, but one of the most important is that ethical and political issues are always emerging. Ethical guidelines, such as

---

Political model of rigour in qualitative research

• Positionality—Research that claims to be objective and uninfluenced by the standpoint of the author is deceptive. Texts must recount the position from which the author speaks.
• Community as arbiter of quality—Academic, political and participant communities become important arbiters of the quality and value of research.
• Voice—Research should provide voice to those who are silenced or marginalised in traditional political processes.
• Critical subjectivity—A reflexive self-awareness is required in order to be able to be sensitive to the voices of others.
• Sacredness—Some researchers seek to re-enchant contemporary life, and see this as an extension of a profound respect for the dignity, justice and collaborative nature of the research process (see also Reason 1993).
• Sharing the privileges—Researchers should aim to acknowledge the importance of participant contributions to their research and return to them both results and, perhaps, royalties! Research should not be written simply for our own benefit and consumption, but also for the participants.
(Summarised from Lincoln 1995.)

---

those produced by various sociological, anthropological and medical bodies, can be useful, but they need to be open to change due to the contingencies of the way research practice and analysis evolves. Ethical issues arise both during data collection and data analysis. Researchers must ask themselves whether their actions, particularly what they write up for publication, genuinely respect the 'other' they are writing about. Laurel Richardson confronts us with the ethical and political dimensions of research when she asks 'How is knowledge created? By and for whom? And with what consequences for individuals, groups, and society?' (1997: 102). Whether research is conducted ethically is not only a procedural matter, decided by committees, but a political and practical matter influenced by how the researcher answers precisely these questions about the impact and consequences of the research for participants.

Summary reflections

Is qualitative research biased? Yes, and no. All research is biased in the sense that all research is integrally political. However, to suggest that something is biased suggests that there is an 'unbiased' interpretation. Feminism, postmodernism and hermeneutics all reject this ideal of identifying 'one true, unbiased' interpretation. I have argued that a more productive way of dealing with the claim of bias is to recognise that all research represents particular political interests and theoretical influences. Bias cannot be avoided, but neither is it something that renders all research simply 'relative'. Rather, researchers must recognise that if they are to be heard by an intended audience, whether this be practitioners, policy makers or other researchers, then the research and written report must engage with the understandings and experiences of these audiences. Only by engaging in dialogue with the preexisting understanding of different audiences, even if you disagree with them, will research be seen as persuasive and have a chance of constructively influencing future theory, policy and practice.

Further reading

Rigour

Altheide, D. and Johnson, J. 1994 'Criteria for assessing
interpretive validity in qualitative research' in N. Denzin
& Y. Lincoln (eds) *Handbook of Qualitative Research*,
Thousand Oaks, Sage, pp. 485–99.
Bishop, R. 1998 'Freeing ourselves from neo-colonial domination
in research: a Maori approach to creating knowledge'
International Journal of Qualitative Studies in Education,
vol. 11, no. 2, pp. 199–221.
Lincoln, Y. 1995 'Emerging criteria for quality in qualitative and
interpretive research' *Qualitative Inquiry*, vol. 1, no. 3,
pp. 275–89.
Manning, K. 1997 'Authenticity in constructivist inquiry'
Qualitative Inquiry, vol. 3, no. 1, pp. 93–116.
Mishler, E. 1990 'Validation in inquiry-guided research:
the role of exemplars in narrative studies'
Harvard Educational Review, vol. 60, no. 3, pp. 415–42.

Constructing policy-oriented research

Patton, M. 1990 *Qualitative Evaluation and Research Methods*,
2nd edn, Newbury Park, Sage.
Rist, R. 1994 'Influencing the policy process with qualitative
research' in N. Denzin and Y. Lincoln (eds)
Handbook of Qualitative Research, Thousand Oaks, Sage,
pp. 545–58.
Travers, M. 1997 'Preaching to the converted? Improving the
persuasiveness of criminal justice research' *British Journal
of Criminology*, vol. 37, no. 2, pp. 359–77.

Politics as part of research

Becker, H. and Horowitz, I. 1972 'Radical politics and
sociological research: observations on methodology and
ideology' *American Journal of Sociology*, vol. 78, no. 1,
pp. 48–66.

Mies, M. 1991 'Women's research or feminist research?' in M. Fonow and J. Cook (eds) *Beyond Methodology: Feminist Scholarship as Lived Research*, Bloomington, IN, Indiana University Press, pp. 60–84.

Discussions of the ethical and political consequences of research for participants

Dickson, G. 2000 '"Aboriginal grandmothers" experience with health promotion and participatory action research' *Qualitative Health Research*, vol. 10, no. 2, pp. 188–213.

Oakley, A. 1998 'Gender, methodology and people's ways of knowing' *Sociology*, vol. 34, no. 4, pp. 707–31.

Richardson, L. 1992 'Trash on the corner: ethics and ethnography' *Journal of Contemporary Ethnography*, vol. 21, no. 1, pp. 103–19.

3

Data analysis during data collection

Openness to transformation means openness to *the local contingencies* that complicate one's agenda and may even force one to reset or abandon one's priorities. The contingencies of field inquiry are not to be viewed only as obstacles to one's inquiries but as opportunities to learn which inquiries are the ones that really matter. These contingencies should be celebrated, for they are where all real discoveries lie (Liberman 1999: 50).

'Can you help me? I am conducting a qualitative study and have collected all my data on topic X and I'm not sure what to do with it now. How should I analyse it?' This is my version of an occasional, but regular, request that appears on some of the qualitative email lists I subscribe to. This sort of request typically comes from a novice qualitative researcher, newly subscribed to the list. The answer to this question is that if you have been collecting your data carefully you have already begun to analyse the data. Hopefully the person has already begun to think about what they are interested in and what issues those data have raised. This provides the beginning of data analysis.

Data analysis in most qualitative research begins during data collection. This practice is consistent with the theory of data analysis discussed in Chapter 1 that emphasised the dialectical, or hermeneutic, relationship between theory and data. This chapter reviews the practicalities of integrating data analysis and data collection. Many texts on qualitative data analysis begin their discussion with what to do *after* data have been collected. If data analysis begins only after the data have been collected, researchers will have missed many valuable opportunities that can be taken only *at the same time* as they are collecting their data. This is particularly the case if you are using the methodology of grounded theory. However, it also applies more generally to most other research methods that are interpretive, inductive and exploratory.

Waiting until after data have been collected to begin data analysis can lead to some significant problems during data analysis. If researchers leave the decision about what sort of data analysis they want to conduct until after they collect their data, they may have precluded, or made difficult, certain types of data analysis. For example, it is difficult to conduct a narrative analysis if the researcher asks short, directed questions that cut off the interviewee. Further, during data analysis the researcher will typically discover and notice unanticipated issues that have arisen early in the data collection. If data analysis is left until afterwards these issues will not be noticed during data collection; they will therefore not be pursued during the data collection and cannot be pursued in any depth during the data analysis.

This chapter does not attempt to review all possible methods of data collection. There are numerous books that have described these processes well, and interested readers are referred to books such as Kellehear (1993), Mason (1996), Daly et al. (1997), Denzin (1997) and Rice and Ezzy (1999). Rather, this chapter focuses on conducting data analysis while the data collection is being undertaken.

Integrating data collection and data analysis

The integration and interpenetration of data collection and data analysis is practised by a number of qualitative research traditions, including ethnography (Rosaldo 1989), participatory action research (Nelson et al. 1998) and grounded theory (Strauss 1987). Simultaneous data collection and data analysis builds on the strengths of qualitative methods as an inductive method for building theory and interpretations from the perspective of the people being studied. It allows the analysis to be shaped by the participants in a more fundamental way than if analysis is left until after the data collection has been finished. Renato Rosaldo describes the method of interpretive ethnographers as follows:

Ethnographers beginning research with a set of questions, revise them throughout the course of inquiry, and in the end emerge with different questions than they started with. One's surprise at the answer to a question, in other words, requires one to revise the question until lessening surprises or diminishing returns indicate a stopping point (Rosaldo 1989: 7).

Theoretical questions, and answers, are shaped and reshaped in an ongoing dialogue with the experience or subjects being studied. Rosaldo began his research of Ilongot subsistence farmers in the Philippines, searching for an explanation for what motivated them to headhunt. He did not accept their claim that it was an expression of their rage associated with bereavement and looked for some other, 'deeper', reason. However, as his fieldwork progressed, and with his own experience of bereavement following the death of his wife due to an accident, Rosaldo came to understand both what the Ilongots meant by rage in bereavement, and shifted the focus of his questioning from headhunting to the experience of bereavement. Examining the implications of his data for his research questions *during* his fieldwork led Rosaldo to modify his research questions, which in turn provided him with a much more sophisticated understanding of the experience he had set out to study.

One of the central canons of grounded theory is that data collection and data analysis are interrelated processes (Glaser &

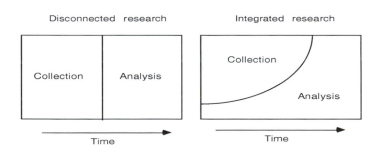

Figure 3.1 Relationships between data analysis and data collection
(Adapted from Lofland & Lofland 1971: 132.)

Strauss 1967; Becker 1971; Strauss & Corbin 1990): 'In grounded theory, the analysis begins as soon as the first bit of data is collected' (Corbin & Strauss 1990: 6). In grounded theory, data collected early in the research process are used to guide the questions that are asked as the research progresses. Data gathered early in a research project guide both the formulation of concepts and the sampling process (a technique referred to as theoretical sampling, described below). Grounded theory is conducted this way because it is assumed that researchers will not know all the important research questions, sampling dimensions or theoretical concepts before they begin collecting data (see the section on grounded theory in Chapter 1). The research questions, the sampling frame and the theoretical concepts are discovered only while the data are being collected:

> Each investigator enters the field with some questions or areas for observation, or will soon generate them. Data will be collected on these matters throughout the research endeavour, unless the questions prove, during analysis to be irrelevant. In order *not* to miss anything that may be salient, however, the investigator must analyse the first bits of data for cues. All seemingly relevant issues must be incorporated into the next set of interviews and observations (Strauss & Corbin 1990: 6).

Examining data right from the beginning of data collection for 'cues' is what makes grounded theory 'grounded'. It is also the foundation of inductive theory building. Data collection is guided either by preconceived theories and ideas about what is important, or data collection is guided by the cues that present themselves during the data collection process. As was argued in Chapter 1, a sophisticated understanding of theory building recognises that interpretations are a product of both previous understandings and the influence of events in the world. Ethnography, hermeneutics and grounded theory all emphasise this interweaving of theory and data.

Postmodernist and poststructuralist thought can be seen as at least partially consistent with this understanding of the interpenetration of data collection and analysis (Becker & McCall 1990; Denzin 1997). Postmodernists argue, for example, that research reports should be seen more as contributions to ongoing conversations about a research issue rather than as final analyses of 'the truth' (Lather 1993). It could be argued that the postmodernist point that preexisting theory and interpretations influence the data collection process is simply a more sophisticated way of describing what grounded theorists have been doing for some time. Game (1991) argues that mainstream sociology and poststructuralist practice seem incompatible because sociology emphasises objectivity, and the independence of the researcher, whereas poststructuralist semiotics emphasises the interpenetration of meaning and experience. While this criticism is true of much sociological research, particularly the demographic and statistical research characteristic of mainstream American sociology, it is not an accurate analysis of qualitative sociological research, particularly research within the interpretive or symbolic interactionist tradition. As Becker & McCall (1990) observe, symbolic interactionists emphasise that, in order to understand social life, researchers must examine the meanings that shape the processes of interaction. The situated, interpretive and processual emphasis of symbolic interactionists has many similarities to the practice of poststructuralists. There are, however, some significant differences between these two approaches, for example in relation to their understanding of the role of political and ethical questions in the research process (see the discussion of rigour in Chapter 2). Nonetheless, they both argue that research practice should explicitly combine the processes of data collection and analysis.

The aim of qualitative research is to allow the voice of the 'other', of the people being researched, to inform the researcher. The finite nature of human perception means that researchers always choose to focus on one or another aspect of a phenomenon. The voice of the participant, rather than the voice of the researcher, will be heard best when participants not only provide the data to be analysed, but when they also contribute to the questions that frame the research and contribute to the way the data are analysed. One way of achieving this is by ensuring the interpenetration of data collection and data analysis.

Techniques for integrating analysis and collection

This section describes a number of practical techniques that can be utilised alongside qualitative interviewing to begin the data analysis process. Long interviews are one of the most common methods of data collection utilised by qualitative researchers, both as a method on their own and as part of other methods, such as ethnography or participatory action research. Here I do not describe the techniques of interviewing: there is a wide variety of excellent books that describe in detail the method and process of long interviews (Holstein & Gubrium 1995; Rubin & Rubin 1995). Rather I describe a number of techniques that can be utilised during data collection, using interviewing as an example, that facilitate the concurrent analysis of data while they are being collected (see text box below).

Techniques for data analysis concurrent with early data collection

- Team meetings and peer debriefing.
- Checking interpretations with participants.
- Transcribing, reading and coding early data.
- Writing journals and memos.

Team meetings and peer debriefing

In 1997 I led a team of three researchers interviewing people living with HIV/AIDS about how they understood their future (Ezzy 2000a). After each researcher had conducted one or two interviews we had a team meeting to discuss our progress. One member had interviewed a person with hepatitis C. While discussing this interview it became apparent that co-infection with hepatitis C significantly influenced the experience of living with HIV/AIDS. A question about hepatitis C was therefore added to our theme list after the first few interviews. In this way, the interview theme list was updated continually during the data collection for this project as new topics and new emphases were identified in the interviews and then discussed in team meetings. Most of the data analysis for this project was conducted after the interviews were complete. However, discussing the research while data collection was being conducted allowed a preliminary analysis of the data. As a consequence the research was able to adapt and include previously unanticipated dimensions of the experience of living with HIV/AIDS.

Anselm Strauss is perhaps one of the most accomplished collaborative qualitative researchers of the twentieth century (Maines 1991). As such, his discussion of team meetings as part of the research process is worth reading carefully if you are involved in a collective qualitative project (Strauss 1987). Strauss suggests that team meetings should be taped, transcribed, and included in the memo files of the research project. Strauss identifies four main benefits from team meetings. First, discussing the data of the research stimulates ideas about its meaning and significance. Second, some issues that arise during the discussion are elaborated and developed that provide additional depth of complexity and quality of analysis to the research. Third, the issues raised may lead to team members choosing to follow up issues through new data collection, the addition of questions to the research schedule, or reviewing data collected earlier for an analysis of the issues raised. Finally, team discussions may inform the writing up of the project, particularly if they are transcribed. Regular team discussions force researchers to confront common research issues and encourage a focus on similar lines of inquiry. The development of a shared analytic framework during data collection makes writing up team research considerably easier. Using team meetings to work the tensions between individual interests and the team project can lead to a healthy development of both: 'In terms of the forward thrust of the entire project team discussions not only ensure commonality of perspective, but also the possibility of individual growth and a measure of autonomy in the further pursuit of ideas: pursuit—it is important to emphasize—within the common framework of analysis' (Strauss 1987: 139). Backett-Milburn and associates' (1999) reflection on a collaborative feminist research project similarly points out that negotiation and compromise is required if the differences between team members' interests and positions are to lead to a stimulating synergy rather than dispiriting arguments.

For the solo researcher, peer debriefings can provide similar benefits to team meetings. Peer debriefing is 'the process of exposing oneself to a disinterested peer in a manner paralleling an analytic session and for the purpose of exploring aspects of the inquiry that might otherwise remain only implicit within the inquirer's mind' (Lincoln & Guba 1985: 308). Spall (1998) suggests that peer debriefing should be conducted at crucial junctures during the research and that it has three main benefits. First, it makes the researchers more aware of the influence of their personal values and theoretical orientations on the collection and interpretation of the data. This point also includes discussions of issues that may be ethically or legally problematic. Second, debriefing sessions provide researchers with an opportunity to explore and test their theories and interpretations of the data through discussion with a colleague familiar with their discipline. Finally, debriefing allows researchers to discuss problems with, and planning of, the methodology.

Below is an example of how debriefing can inform the research process. It is a personal communication in response to a paper I have published on the experience of unemployment (Ezzy 2000b). Although it is not the result of a debriefing session, it elegantly illustrates the sort of information that a debriefing can provide to the researcher. In her response to my paper, Henshaw discusses the different ways in which respondents portrayed themselves in interviews. Some told stories describing themselves as in control, others recounted victim narratives. In the paper I point out that some respondents reported telling different types of stories to different audiences. However, I do not really explore the question of what type of 'audience' I, the researcher, might have been for the participant:

> In short, you have not relayed to the reader the exact context of who you are in relation to your interviewees, nor indicated how they might have viewed you. For example, if you were perceived to be 'an authority from an important university', your interviewees might have had a vested interest in presenting themselves in the best possible light. On the other hand, you might have been a complete stranger and provided them with a great deal of space to represent themselves in whichever way they wished . . . Therefore, because you have not made the relationship (i.e., yourself as the context) between you and your participants quite clear enough, the reader has some confusion about where to situate the veracity of your observations (S. Henshaw, personal communication).

Henshaw's criticism of my paper is justified, and in response I could provide more information about how I presented myself, as an interviewer, to the interviewee. Unfortunately Henshaw's analysis came after the paper was published, but it nonetheless illustrates the value of obtaining peer debriefing not only on draft papers but also on all aspects of the research process. Research reports, including journal articles and books, are a contribution to an ongoing dialogue and debate within academic, political and participant communities. Understanding does not come only from individual researchers locking themselves away and reflecting on their data. The responses of others to our interpretations are a central part of the process of developing a trustworthy account. Team meetings and peer debriefings provide a valuable opportunity to begin this dialogue with other researchers early in the research process.

Checking interpretations with participants

Later in this chapter I discuss the suggestion that research participants should be included in all aspects of the research process. Feminists and participatory action researchers have pointed out that this has important emancipatory political implications for the research process. However, it also provides a mechanism for developing the dialogue with the research participant that is at the heart of the qualitative research process. Whether or not participants are involved from the beginning, in the design of the research or as members of a steering committee, it is important to consider how evolving interpretations of the data can be checked with participants. Lather and Smithies (1997) asked participants to read drafts of their research reports. In my own research I try to integrate data collection by checking my evolving interpretations with participants.

The aim of a good in-depth interview is to obtain the story or interpretation of the person being interviewed. From this perspective it is important not to try to suggest to the person how you, as the interviewer, might expect them to respond. This is not an argument for being neutral, it is an argument for ensuring that the interviewer genuinely listens to the voice of the interviewee (Rice & Ezzy 1999). However, during a long interview I typically begin to develop my own summary of the interviewee's experience. I begin to place the person's experience in the emerging theory that I have about the issues being studied. Towards the end of my interviews I often ask people about this interpretation that I have developed of their experience. This serves as a check on whether I have understood what they are saying. For example, in my study of unemployment and mental health I identified a link between a number of factors. People who felt confident about the future, even though unemployed, also typically expressed dissatisfaction with the job they had left or lost, and were financially secure at least for the short term. This positive orientation to unemployment was a product of both the person's social location and a product of the type of story he or she told about the experience. The following extract is an example from one of my interviews that illustrates how I examined this link by discussing it with one of my participants at the end of the interview. Gail was a single mother in her forties who had been working full-time as a teacher, but who also had a contract to write a book. She saw her time of unemployment as an opportunity to finish writing her book.

Doug:	Can I just check with you if my understanding is correct?
Gail:	Sure. [Laughs]
Doug:	It seems to me that you were a little bit frustrated with the work you were doing at the hospital.
Gail:	Yeah, frustrated a lot, not a little bit.
Doug:	When the position finished and they redeployed you, you wanted to get out. Financially it is attractive to you because you have got the redundancy package.
Gail:	Reasonably attractive. Don't let's get carried away too much with the value. It is not that much money.
Doug:	And that you feel moderately financially secure for a short while?
Gail:	[Laughs] Yes, a very short while.
Doug:	But more importantly, you feel confident that you can get work in the future if you need to support yourself financially.
Gail:	Yeah, but that could be a false confidence, don't forget.
Doug:	I mean, do you feel confident or not?
Gail:	Well, if I worry now about not getting a job, I am going to start applying for jobs now and put all my energy into looking for another job, which will deflect from my work on my book. So whether I am using denial so that I don't worry about it or whether I am confident about it probably doesn't matter very much at all. Let's just say that I am confident!
Doug:	I understand.

This extract elegantly illustrates the usefulness of this sort of checking with the participant. It demonstrates that Gail is aware of several different possible interpretations of her current experience. She could begin to worry about the future. This would lead her into searching for another job and, as a consequence, she would not be able to finish her book. However, she has chosen instead to interpret her situation in a way that provides her with

some self-confidence. Checking my interpretation of her experience with her at the end of the interview brought out the nature
of her experience in a clearer light than would otherwise have
been the case.

Some researchers advocate returning transcripts of interviews
to interviewees for checking (Mason 1996). This may be a useful
strategy for checking details of the interview. A similar strategy is
to send participants summary vignettes that the researcher
has prepared from their interviews (Lather & Smithies 1997).
A summary vignette, through the process of selection, contains
preliminary data analysis. Checking a summary vignette with a
participant allows the participant to engage with the researcher as
they are doing their data analysis. The participant may point to
under- or overemphases and suggest complexities that were not
originally envisaged.

Transcribing, reading and coding early data

There is a temptation—that should be resisted—when conducting
long interviews to leave transcribing the interviews until after data
collection is complete. This is particularly the case if the researcher
has some funds allocated to having the tapes transcribed. It is
easier to leave transcription to be organised all at the one time.
However, there is considerable value to be obtained from
researchers themselves transcribing the first couple of interviews
they conduct before conducting the remaining interviews. First,
this allows interviewers to observe themselves in action, which can
be both painful and enlightening. As I transcribed my first interview, I remember saying to myself: 'Did I really say that?'. It was a
painful experience as I noted how I cut the participant off in the
middle of an account, and completely missed a cue on an important issue. Second, transcribing the interview takes considerable
time, and encourages detailed reflection on the issues of the
research. I also began jotting down notes and ideas about theories
and concepts while transcribing the interview. Transcription
served as a preliminary form of data analysis. I began to make
links between the experience of the participants and concepts and
theory. Irvine (1999), in her exemplary study of Codependents
Anonymous, describes a similar process during her fieldwork utilising participant observation. Note-taking fed directly into the
process of data analysis.

In the initial stages of my fieldwork I developed simple codes from my notes from meetings. At first I coded what appeared to be parts of the meeting, such as 'Setting up', 'Leading', 'Speaking' and 'Sharing'. Before long I began to develop more sophisticated codes within each of these coded categories. For example, within 'Speaking' and 'Sharing', I developed codes for 'Dysfunctional Childhood', 'Abuse', 'Hitting Bottom' and 'First Steps in Recovery', among others (Irvine 1999: 13).

These codes were then compared against ongoing observation, so that Irvine's theoretical coding scheme developed alongside her data collection. The two-way process of data collection and data analysis allowed Irvine both to develop a more sophisticated theoretical model and to collect data that were relevant to her research questions and evolving theoretical scheme. Coding is discussed in more detail in Chapter 4, but it is important to underline the value of beginning the coding process during data collection.

Journals and memos

Write [your fieldnotes] as lushly as you can, as loosely as you can, as long as you put yourself into it, where you say 'I felt that' (though not to too great a degree). And as loose as that lush adverbalized prose is, it's still a richer matrix to start from than stuff that gets reduced into a few words of 'sensible' sentences . . . you've go to start by trusting yourself and writing as fully and lushly as you can (Goffman 1989: 131).

Many researchers advocate developing a sophisticated filing system from the beginning of data collection as the foundation of the data analysis process (Lofland & Lofland 1971; Strauss & Corbin 1990). This filing system can include a variety of memos or journals on the practicalities of conducting fieldwork and emergent interpretations of the significance of data collected for the project as a whole. Journals and memos are a systematic attempt to facilitate the interpretive process that is at the heart of qualitative research. Understandings, interpretations and theories do not emerge from data through some mechanical process. They are a product of researchers thinking and talking about their research. Keeping a journal and regularly writing memos encourages researchers to reflect routinely on their emerging understanding of the data.

Writing memos is particularly central to grounded theory, as it forms the foundation of the emergent coding scheme. Strauss defines a theoretical memo as 'writing in which the researcher puts down theoretical question, hypotheses, summary of codes, etc.— a method of keeping track of coding results and stimulating further coding, and also a major means for integrating the theory' (1987: 22). Most grounded theorists write memos regularly, typically from the beginning of the research project, as part of both data collection and data analysis, which occur concurrently.

Looking back over my journals and memos from several research projects, there is a pattern in how they develop that is similar to the pattern described by Strauss (1987). My journals begin with questions, suggestions about what I expect to find, and ideas for reading. They move through notes that remind me of people I should talk to about my findings, suggestions for sampling, detailed discussions of particular interviews, and thoughts about how particular books I was reading might relate to the interview material. They also contain attempts to develop categories and concepts, linking these to particular participants or observations. Towards the end of the journal I begin to focus more on the structure of the analysis as a whole and how particular cases might fit into, or suggest modifications to, this structure.

The memo on Michelle (see text box, p. 73) is an example of how theory and categories for data analysis emerge during the writing of memos during data collection. The memo was written quite soon after the interview, probably after I had transcribed the tape. In the memo I develop an emerging theory of what factors might influence how people respond to losing their job. The theory is not fully developed; it is after all only a memo early in the research. But it contains an indication of the theory I later developed of the different ways that people respond to job loss (Ezzy 2000b). In contrast to the interview with Gail reported earlier, Michelle was distressed, and the memo suggests that this might be linked to the importance of working among her friends and the pleasure she found in her last job. However, the memo also suggests that she was not as distressed as some other interviewees (one of whom was suicidal) and links this to her being active, not having friends at her last workplace, and being financially supported by her parents.

Michelle: a memo

A very unpleasant job loss—no notice:
— implication that she was worthless
— enjoyed the work
— stopped her obtaining her traineeship certificate.
But:
— no friends at last workplace
— involved in dancing and public speaking and this helped
(cf. journal page 7).
Note that all her important friends are working. This contributes to the maintenance of her own understanding of work as central to her future. The social construction of identity.
Working is also central to her understanding of a satisfying future, even if she has children at some stage.
Unemployment leads to a loss of direction (interview transcript page 3).
Depressed, angry and frustrated, but not suicidal.
Kept spirits up by active job search, regular activities such as dancing and public speaking, which provide a sense of achievement.
Financially dependent on parents. This means she survives financially, but wants the financial independence provided by work.
(From my journal for my study of unemployment Ezzy 2000b).

Qualitative data analysis is an *interpretive* task. Interpretations are not found—rather they are made, actively constructed through social processes. Data collection in qualitative research is not something easily separated off from data analysis. Researchers make many choices during data collection that are integral to how the data are analysed and will be analysed—choices, for example, about what or who to sample, what to ask, what to pursue, and what to ignore. These choices are a product of the researcher's developing interpretation of the phenomena being studied. This interpretive task is the beginning of, and integral to, qualitative data analysis. The interpretive process of analysing qualitative data includes: team meetings and peer debriefing; checking interpretations with participants; transcribing, reading and coding early data; and writing journals and memos. These, along with a variety of other procedures, are ways of building an interpretation of the phenomena through a dialogue with the phenomena and with other people's interpretations of the phenomena. Qualitative researchers should aim to make the interpretive process explicit and integral to their research, right from the beginning of the research.

Sampling and saturation

The most important point about sampling, as it relates to qualitative data analysis, is that the sample is purposeful. The two most common, and undesirable, sampling techniques employed in qualitative research are convenience samples and snowball samples (Patton 1990). The main disadvantage with these methods is that the only rationale is ease or convenience. A purposeful sample is one that provides a clear criterion or rationale for the selection of participants, or places to observe, or events, that relates to the research questions. A wide variety of sampling techniques have been documented in a number of qualitative methodology texts (Miles & Huberman 1994; Rice & Ezzy 1999). A sample that aims for maximum variation, for example, would be most useful if the aim of the research was to document the variations and patterns in a particular phenomenon. Another sampling technique might focus on extreme or deviant cases in order to illustrate processes that would otherwise be difficult to observe. The important point is that the reasons for the sample are clearly related to the research questions. Theoretical sampling, used by grounded theorists, illustrates this link between sampling choices and research questions.

In grounded theory, the units of analysis are sampled on theoretical grounds (Glaser & Strauss 1967; Strauss 1987; Strauss & Corbin 1990). This means that the sample is not defined prior to the research but as the theoretical dimensions emerge during the research. For example, during my research on unemployment I developed a theory that the level of distress experienced by an unemployed person was strongly influenced by the level of financial distress. This theory was developed out of interviews with people on relatively low incomes with and without significant debt. Among these people the level of debt correlated with the level of distress, and formed a central part of their talk about why they were or were not distressed. That is to say, while being poor is not pleasant, it is much more tolerable if you have no debt and have no-one else who is financially dependent on you. I had also interviewed wealthy unemployed people who were not distressed and were living quite comfortably on their income. To examine this proposition more fully, I sought out unemployed people who had a high income while unemployed and also had a sizeable financial debt or considerable financial obligations, such as a large dependent family. These people were distressed both financially and more generally, despite their relatively high level of income. Interviews with them underlined that it was not the absolute level of income but the level of income relative to financial obligations that caused distress. The earlier interviews had also indicated that this was the case, but the theoretical sampling procedure made the argument even stronger. Sampling conducted on theoretical grounds resulted in a more sophisticated understanding of the nature of financial distress experienced by unemployed people.

Theoretical sampling stops when the researcher decides the study has reached saturation. The idea of theoretical saturation was first formally described by Glaser and Strauss (1967). This idea appears to have had its source in Everett Hughes, who advised his students to keep interviewing until they did not hear anything new (Hintz & Miller 1995). To be able to do this requires, of course, that researchers are analysing their data as they are collecting it, otherwise it would be very difficult to identify when saturation had been achieved. This advice has implications both for the sample size and for the types of units sampled. Strauss (1987) observes there will always be new issues that can be pursued. However, data collection has to end at some point, and in theoretical sampling this point is decided on theoretical grounds, as a consequence of concurrent data analysis and data collection.

Including participants in all aspects of the research

Feminist theory highlights the centrality of relationships to the research process: 'Research is an inherently relational process that involves shared stories, actual bodies, and real voices' (Way 1997: 704). Relationships necessarily involve power differentials: 'The prominence given within feminist methodological literature to the importance of understanding what methods "do" both to research participants and to research "findings" has been very important in reconstituting knowledge-claims and in helping to develop a more democratic social science' (Oakley 1998: 725). A more democratic research practice is typically achieved by formally involving the researched as participants in the research process.

Drawing on participatory methodologies, some feminists have included research subjects as co-researchers in their projects. The aim of making subjects co-researchers is to avoid exploiting the 'subjects' and to empower women to research issues that concern them. Lather and Smithies (1997), for example, refer to their 'subjects' as participants or contributors to their research. Rather than taking 'control' of the data once the interviews were completed, they included their participants in the writing process as an 'editorial board' (Lather & Smithies 1997: 215).

Participatory research and feminist research share many objectives and have been utilised together (Maguire 1987). Participatory research developed in response to a similar desire by researchers in developing countries to include participants in the research process (Yeich 1996). Brydon-Miller reports that it was first used in the early 1970s 'by Maria Lissa Swantz to describe work then being conducted in Tanzania that drew on the knowledge and expertise of community members in creating locally controlled development projects' (1997: 658). The research attempts to include participants at every stage of the process: 'They participate in a process of developing research questions, designing research instruments, collecting information, and reflecting on the data in order to transform their understanding about the nature of the problem under investigation' (Nelson et al. 1998: 884).

Morrow and Smith report that during their qualitative focus group study of sexual abuse survivors they invited some participants to become co-analysts during the data analysis phase of the research: 'The 4 coanalysts (termed participant-coresearchers) continued to meet with Morrow for more than a year. They acted as the primary source of participant verification, analysing video-tapes of the group sessions in which they had participated, suggesting categories, and revising the emerging theory and model' (Morrow & Smith 1995: 26).

Involving participants as co-researchers can be challenging, for feminists and non-feminists alike. Not only does it question the traditional presumed expertise of the academic researcher, it requires innovations in data gathering, analysis and writing (Olesen 1994). This can be particularly problematic if, for example, the researcher and the researched do not share similar political objectives, such as a commitment to feminist emancipation.

Formally involving participants as co-researchers is not simply a response to political concerns but also part of a practice that aims to hear the voice of the other, to use the hermeneutic turn of phrase. Feminist methods emphasise the need to 'hear voices', and this draws attention to the human connection: 'to the relationship between speaker and listener, to the possibility of different languages, and thus to the potential for misunderstanding or mistranslation as well as to the ability of people to see and to speak about themselves and the world in more than one way' (Gilligan, quoted in Way 1997: 705).

The extent to which participants are involved in research varies considerably. Many qualitative researchers ask participants to read transcripts of interviews, others include participants on steering committees or as part of a consultative process in designing the research. The degree of involvement reflects, in part, the political orientations of the researcher, and the political objectives of the research. I argue that there are no universally correct standards for acceptable levels of participant inclusion in research projects. My point is that the past practice of reducing the role of participants to merely providing information in interviews will probably provide neither the most useful data nor the optimum political outcomes. The extent of involvement of participants has now become a question that each researcher must address in developing a research plan and practice.

Summary reflections

Most qualitative researchers do not presume to know all their research questions before they start data collection. Additional research questions can be discovered and researched only by conducting data analysis, even if this is of a very preliminary kind, during the process of data collection. Many qualitative researchers do not know the dimensions along which they will sample for their data. These dimensions can be discovered only by conducting preliminary data analysis during data collection, and thus following the practice of theoretical sampling. Many qualitative researchers seek to include participants in all aspects of the research process. Participants can only suggest additional, or different, research questions; or suggest alternative sources of data, if they are provided with, and/or included in, preliminary analyses conducted during the process of data collection.

Qualitative data analysis is a process of interpretation. Data are not interpreted *after* they are collected. Although interpretation does happen after data collection, data collection *itself* is an inter-pretive process. Choices about what to ask and who, or what to sample, are products of interpretive understandings. If the researcher conducts systematic data analysis during data collection, then the process of data collection will be guided not only by the researcher's preexisting interpretations but also by the emerging interpretations of participants.

Conducting data analysis during data collection results in a more sophisticated and subtle analysis of the data. The interpretive process begins when the researcher begins to reflect on his or her research. From this moment data analysis begins, and should be systematically conducted. Doing so will make for an easier, richer, more subtle and more useful analysis.

Further reading

Interviewing

Holloway, W. and Jefferson, T. 1997 'Eliciting narrative through the in-depth interview' *Qualitative Inquiry*, vol. 3, no. 1, pp. 53–71.
Holstein, J. and Gubrium, J. 1995 *The Active Interview*, Thousand Oaks, Sage.
Rubin, H. and Rubin, I. 1995 *Qualitative Interviewing: The Art of Hearing Data*, Thousand Oaks, Sage.

Journals and memos

Mason, J. 1996 *Qualitative Researching*, London, Sage.
Strauss, A. 1987 *Qualitative Analysis for Social Scientists*, Cambridge, Cambridge University Press.
Strauss, A. and Corbin, J. 1990 *Basics of Qualitative Research*, London, Sage.

Empirical studies with good descriptions of their data analysis methodology

Irvine, L. 1999 *Codependent Forevermore: The Invention of Self in a Twelve Step Group*, Chicago, University of Chicago Press.

Lather, P. and Smithies, C. 1997 *Troubling the Angels: Women Living with HIV/AIDS*, Boulder, HarperCollins.

Morrow, S. and Smith, M. 1995 'Constructions of survival and coping by women who have survived childhood sexual abuse' *Journal of Counseling Psychology*, vol. 42, no. 1, pp. 24–34.

Rosaldo, R. 1989 *Culture and Truth*, London, Routledge.

Sampling

Luborsky, M. and Rubinstein, R. 1995 'Sampling in qualitative research' *Research on Aging*, vol. 17, no. 1, pp. 89–113.

Patton, M. 1990 *Qualitative Evaluation and Research Methods*, 2nd edn, Newbury Park, Sage.

4

Coding data and interpreting text: methods of analysis

Traditional research designs have considerable limitations . . . A sort of sympathetic magic seems to be involved, the assumption being that if you go through the motions of science then science will result. But it hasn't . . . Understanding of ordinary behavior has not accumulated; distance has (Erving Goffman, quoted in Manning, P. 1992: 141).

The quantitative, and functionalist, research designs that Goffman refers to as 'traditional' are still present today. Influenced by positivism and the attempt to be 'objective' and 'scientific', many research designs systematically distance the researched from the researcher. As a consequence the researcher is much less likely to 'hear' the 'voice' of the participants. It is relatively easy to conduct a quantitative survey, or a group of one-off qualitative interviews, with a group of participants. It is easier to publish the results of a quantitative survey, takes less time to analyse, and will probably further the career ambitions of the researcher more effectively, depending on his or her disciplinary background. It is much harder to spend time with people listening to their voices, understanding their perspectives and sharing in their problems. Such research is harder to publish, takes more time and energy to conduct, and is often devalued when it comes to career progression. However, this sort of research provides a much more sophisticated understanding of the issues, will facilitate the formulation of more effective policy, and is politically and ethically sensitive.

The problem of overemphasising 'scientific' procedure, and as a consequence using inappropriate methodology, is well illustrated in Tanya Luhrmann's (1989) anthropological ethnography of magic and Witchcraft in contemporary England. The Witch magicians studied by Luhrmann engaged in a variety of magical practices in which they attemped to change physical realities through magical techniques. Luhrmann says that 'the point of the study was to understand how [someone] . . . could come to treat apparently outrageous claims as sensible topics for discussion' (1989: 17). Prior to Luhrmann conducting her research, her participants had been studied by a sociologist, who had handed out questionnaires with categorical questions, and acted as if he was an expert who knew more about the subject than his participants. Questionnaires with fixed response questions are good 'scientific' technique. However, in his quest to follow correct technique this sociologist had completely misunderstood the nature of Witchcraft, and his research report was derided by the Witches as equivalent to an observational study of trees that concluded trees do not grow.

Qualitative researchers study meaning. The quality of research into meanings and interpretive processes can not be assured simply through following correct procedures. Interpretations and meanings are situated. A method applicable to one research situation will be inappropriate in another. Qualitative research is demonstrably trustworthy and rigorous when the researcher demonstrates that he or she has worked to understand the situated nature of participants' interpretations and meanings. The quality of qualitative data analysis depends on following well-thought-out procedures, and on ensuring that these procedures reveal the structures of understanding of participants.

Luhrmann reports that in order to understand the magical practices of Witches she decided that she had to try to share their subjective experience: 'I decided that I would understand magic best if I did what people did to become magicians'. She read, studied and practised magic with a variety of Witches in England. Luhrmann did not hide the fact that she was conducting qualitative research, and this did not worry her participants because she worked hard at fitting in with them. She did not tape-record her conversations or pass out questionnaires, which she thought would only damage her acceptance among the groups in which she participated. She was more interested in understanding the experience of these Witch magicians than in ensuring that she systematically followed a procedure. Luhrmann wanted to understand: 'what it felt like to have a tarot reading, how magicians argued for their practice, what they meant when they said that they "saw" the Goddess. I did not see a complete or representative set of magicians . . . but I did gain considerable participatory insight into the way some people found magic compelling' (1989: 17).

While following correct procedures does not necessarily produce trustworthy qualitative research, this does not mean that qualitative research, and qualitative data analysis in particular, should be completely unsystematic. Phillip Manning identifies three distinct methodological practices in Erving Goffman's work: '(1) metaphor; (2) unsystematic observation; and (3) systematic observation' (1992: 141). The strength of Goffman's analyses lies in his ability to move between practices that provide interpretive understanding, such as metaphor, and practices that provide convincing evidence, based on systematic observations. This mixture of practices is an art that results in research that is both evocative, in the sense that it produces new insight, and convincing, because it rests on systematic research.

This chapter reviews four analytic strategies: content analysis, thematic analysis and grounded theory, narrative analysis, and cultural studies methodology. Clearly these do not exhaust the possible analytic strategies available to qualitative researchers. There are a number of other analytic strategies described in the literature, including phenomenological methods (Moustakas 1994) and conversation analysis (Potter 1996). I have focused on the most commonly utilised methods, aiming to provide an overview of the variety and extent of the available analytic strategies. Discussion of each analytic strategy focuses on practical examples from published research.

Content analysis

Content analysis is the most deductive of all forms of data analysis discussed in this chapter. Deductively derived theory and deductively driven data analysis work 'down' from preexisting theoretical understandings (Glaser & Strauss 1967). The categories of analysis are developed through logical deduction from the preexisting theory. In this way preexisting theory is tested against empirical data. Content analysis begins with predefined categories. Thematic analysis, discussed below, allows categories to emerge from the data.

For example, feminist theory argues that the oppression of women is partly the product of a culture that systematically presents stereotyped images of men and women. From this general theory, categories can be deduced of what constitutes stereotypical images of men and women. A content analysis to test this theory could, for example, examine images of men and women in popular magazines, counting the number of times images of men and women conform to stereotypical roles. A content analysis of Australian popular magazines that employed precisely this method found that popular magazines are 'still presenting stereotyped gender roles, lifestyles, and body management' (Ring 1997: 3).

Content analysis, as with any other form of data analysis, begins with the identification of the population from which units are sampled. A sample is then drawn, typically using some form of stratified sampling (Rice & Ezzy 1999). For example, an American study of representations of masculinity in school textbooks identified children's reading books utilised in schools as their population (Evans & Davies 2000). Evans and Davies then sampled, or selected, two series of children's textbooks published by two different publishers. They then selected first-grade, third-grade and fifth-grade books to provide a distribution of ages of intended readers.

Content analysis next defines the units of analysis and the categories into which these will be placed. Evans and Davies used characters in the stories as their units of analysis. Before their analysis they developed an 'instrument' for categorising the characters based on a inventory developed for classifying personality traits in children's stories. They identified eight stereotypical masculine traits and eight stereotypical feminine traits and developed definitions of these traits *before* beginning their analysis. For example, Evans and Davies define the stereotypical masculine trait of aggression as 'actions and motives with intent to hurt or frighten; imparts hostile feelings' (2000: 261). Similarly, they define the stereotypical feminine trait of *affection* as 'openly expressing warm feelings; hugging, touching, holding'.

Data analysis involves reviewing each unit of analysis and categorising it according to the predefined categories. The occurrences are then counted and comparisons made, often using statistical or quantitative methods. Evans and Davies reviewed each character portrayed in the stories and identified which of the sixteen traits they portrayed. They then tabulated their results. They found, not surprisingly, that males were portrayed with the stereotypically male characteristics and females with the stereotypically female characteristics. For example, 24 per cent of the male characters demonstrated aggression, compared to only 4 per cent of the female characters. Similarly, 33 per cent of the female characters demonstrated affection, against only 18 per cent of the male characters. Chi-square statistical tests were used to demonstrate the statistical significance of these differences.

The final stage of content analysis is the interpretation of results. Results are compared with the predictions of the pre-existing theory and conclusions for the theory are drawn. In Evans and Davies' case, while very few female characters demonstrated aggression, a significant number of male characters demonstrated affection. This might suggest that, while children's fiction does present stereotypically gendered characters, there are examples that counter the stereotypes. However, this is not the case. Here Evans and Davies resort to a form of thematic analysis, because they identify themes in their data that they had not specified prior to conducting their research. Specifically, they noticed that whenever a male exhibited feminine traits, he did so as part of some socially unacceptable behaviour. Boys who exhibited feminine traits were 'sissy' and derided for showing too much interest in domestic chores, or for wanting to play with girls, or for expressing an interest in quiet play rather than aggressive play. In short, Evans and Davies (2000) report that masculine stereotypes in American schoolbooks are portrayed in the same manner they were twenty years ago. This analysis of gender stereotypes is consistent with Gergen's (1992) content analysis of best-selling American autobiographies, but contrasts with Jagger's (1998) content analysis of dating advertisements, which found that gender stereotypes may be changing with body image and lifestyle choice may now be more important than previously central financial and occupational attributes.

Content analysis is a useful way of confirming or testing a pre-existing theory. When the research question is clearly defined and the categories of analysis have been well established by preexisting research, content analysis may be an extremely useful method of data analysis. It is not, however, a very useful way of building new theory.

Content analysis

- Identify categories prior to searching for them in the data.
- Select the sample to be categorised and identify units of analysis.
- Count, or systematically log, the number of times the categories occur.

(Adapted from Kellehear 1993.)

As the example from Evans and Davies suggests, when new theories or interpretations are required the researcher typically requires a more inductive methodology such as thematic analysis. To explain that masculine characters with apparently feminine traits were not representatives of a new masculinity but derided male 'sissy' characters, Evans and Davies utilised thematic analysis to identify the category of sissy male inductively from the data.

Content analysis assumes that the researcher knows what the important categories will be prior to the analysis. It restricts the extent to which the data are allowed to 'speak' to the researcher. Put another way, it severely limits the extent to which the 'other' can have a voice as part of the research process. For this reason, in qualitative research content analysis tends to be used in conjunction with other forms of data analysis that are more inductive and sensitive to emergent categories and interpretations.

Content analysis can be useful as a stage of data analysis as it allows the relevance of preexisting theory to be tested, and it can be used as a way of assessing the applicability of a theory that emerges during thematic or content analysis. Grounded theorists sometimes use content analysis in this way (Strauss 1987; Strauss & Corbin 1990). Strauss, for example, reports that emergent hypotheses are 'checked out' or 'verified' (1987: 16) during the analysis both through searching for new data and through going back over old data and recoding them according to the new categories. This is, of course, a variation on content analysis.

The skills acquired through learning to conduct content analysis form the basis of many of the skills of the more inductive forms of research, such as thematic analysis and semiotics. The novice qualitative researcher should first learn, and become thoroughly familiar with, the principles of content analysis. This will provide a solid foundation for successfully completing other forms of qualitative analysis.

Coding in thematic analysis and grounded theory

'In short, coding is the process of defining what the data are all about' (Charmaz 1995: 37). Coding in thematic analysis and grounded theory is the process of identifying themes or concepts that are in the data. The researcher attempts to build a systematic account of what has been observed and recorded. Theory emerges through this coding process. Coding links the data to an emergent theory. In this section I use my own research with people with HIV/AIDS to illustrate the various types of coding typically utilised in thematic analysis and grounded theory.

Coding is an easy process that most people have already performed. For example, as an undergraduate I used to use a simple coding method when I was writing undergraduate essays. I would start preparing to write the essay two or three weeks before it was due, reading all the relevant chapters and articles. Then, typically on the night before it was due, I would start writing the essay by reading through all my notes. I would usually have two or three pages of notes on each reference, and perhaps a dozen different references. As I was reading through my notes I would notice that there was a discussion of the same topic in two different readings. So I would call this topic number 1. For example, in an essay about the experience of unemployment, I found several readings focusing on the different stages that unemployed people go through after losing their job (Ezzy 1993). As I continued reading through my notes I would notice other common themes or topics. A number of studies of unemployment, for example, focused on the secondary 'functions' of employment that are lost when a person becomes unemployed. I would code this topic number 2. Eventually I would assign most of my notes with codes that linked them to one or another of my topics. After my first reading through I would go back and find the uncoded bits of notes and try to work out whether they fitted into my existing topics or required a new topic, or could be left out of the essay. Next I would write down all my topics on a piece of paper and rearrange them until I thought I had an argument. I would then write my essay based on the list of topics and my coded notes.

Perhaps you write essays differently? It doesn't really matter. What I want to demonstrate is that coding and categorising is something most people have already performed in tasks as simple as writing notes in the margins of books and articles. Coding in qualitative data analysis is more complex than this, partly because most qualitative researchers work with much larger sets of data. However, the process is similar. The initial identification of topics, often referred to as open coding, is exploratory, looking in the data for codes. As the coding scheme becomes more developed new forms of coding, referred to as axial and selective coding, are used that enable the development of an argument, or central story, around which the research report is organised.

Thematic analysis is part of the early procedures of data analysis in grounded theory, but grounded theory goes beyond thematic analysis. The term 'grounded theory' should be used only to refer to studies in which data collection and data analysis are conducted concurrently alongside theoretical sampling and other techniques distinctive of grounded theory, such as the constant comparative method (Strauss & Corbin 1990). Green observes that many published qualitative research papers routinely parrot the phrase that 'the data were analysed during grounded theory' (1998: 1064). This suggests that a sophisticated procedure has been followed. However, Green points out that results presented in the paper often suggest that the data analysis has utilised only thematic analysis and not the sophisticated methodology of grounded theory: 'Unfortunately, what follows may be merely an account of some key themes in the data, with brief textual quotes in illustration, and sceptical readers remain unconvinced that qualitative analysis is anything other than journalistic reportage' (Green 1998: 1064). The more straightforward procedures of thematic analysis may be appropriate for some studies, but it is important that the researcher clearly identify which data analysis methods have been utilised.

Both thematic analysis and grounded theory employ similar techniques for analysing data. One difference between the two is that grounded theory utilises theoretical sampling in which emerging analysis guides the collection of further data (see the discussion of sampling in Chapter 2), and this is not done in thematic analysis. Grounded theorists have also developed a sophisticated methodology for the development of codes, particularly in relation to the development of core codes during selective coding, and again this is not necessarily done in thematic analysis. Thematic analysis can be employed either as part of a grounded theory analysis or for the analysis of data that have already been entirely collected. In this section I discuss the practice of coding qualitative data, initially reviewing grounded theory and thematic analysis together where they share similar methodologies, then moving to a discussion that focuses on the more sophisticated techniques unique to grounded theory.

Thematic analysis aims to identify themes within the data. Thematic analysis is more inductive than content analysis because the categories into which themes will be sorted are not decided prior to coding the data. These categories are 'induced' from the data. While the general issues that are of interest are determined prior to the analysis, the specific nature of the categories and themes to be explored are not predetermined. This means that this form of research may take the researcher into issues and problems he or she had not anticipated.

A clear example of thematic analysis is provided by Crisp (2000), who designed a qualitative study of persons with disabilities focusing on their interaction with health and rehabilitation professionals. He was particularly interested in examining the different ways people with disabilities respond to, and perceive, health and rehabilitation professionals. Crisp recruited 35 disabled people whom he interviewed using a semi-structured format; he then transcribed these interviews. Within the parameters of his general research question Crisp inspected the data, using thematic analysis techniques, to develop a typology of responses to rehabilitation professionals. The categories of analysis were not defined prior to the analysis, but emerged during the analysis. Crisp reports that at the beginning of his data analysis the 'data was inspected to elicit the conditions that underlie life events, interactions with others, strategies and tactics that are adopted by respondents, and consequences. It was initially coded openly by scrutinising interview transcripts line by line or word by word; by looking for in-vivo codes, terms used by respondents; and by making comparisons for similarities and differences between events and incidents' (2000: 358).

The first stage of coding during thematic analysis and of grounded theory is often described as *open coding*, as suggested in the quote from Crisp in the previous paragraph. Glaser describes open coding as a way to 'generate an emergent set of categories and their properties' (1978: 56). More specifically, Strauss and Corbin describe open coding as 'the part of analysis that pertains specifically to the naming and categorizing of phenomena through close examination of data' (1990: 62). Orona puts it more graphically when she suggests that 'coding each line is the guts' of grounded theory (1990: 1249).

For example, during my research with people living with HIV/AIDS (Ezzy 2000a), as I read through my data the first time, I made notes in the margins beside the following lines from my interviews:

> 'I have only got a couple of years to go . . .'
> 'I was determined to live for ever . . .'
> 'The future was I was dying.'
> 'The future is still unknown to me . . .'
> 'The life expectancy was anything from 5 to 10 years . . .'
> 'That was living for the moment.'
> 'I was just waiting around to die . . .'

The notes in the margins of the interview transcripts highlighted the importance of the future and planning, and how a changed understanding of the length of their life had affected participants. As I read through these marginal notations I noticed a theme emerging about how people thought about time. I then relabelled all these lines with the code 'temporality' and wrote a memo to myself noting that the code 'temporality' could be further broken down depending on differences in the way people were oriented towards the future. That is to say, I noted an emergent theme of time. All the interviews contained a similar theme linked to their concern about how people living with HIV/AIDS understood the temporal nature of their lives. I named this theme with the code 'temporality'. Some people were confident, expecting that they would live out a normal lifetime. Others expected to die soon, and were angry or depressed as a consequence. A third group of participants expected their life to be shorter, but had accepted this and celebrated the life that they had (Ezzy 2000a).

Open coding often involves considerable experimentation. At first I experimented with the code 'future orientation'. However, I realised that the issue was not just how people thought about the future but included how people felt about the present, given what they expected to happen in the future. I experimented with a variety of conceptual labels, or categories, or codes (all these words mean the same sort of thing), until I found codes that seemed to fit the data.

This process sounds very straightforward. However, it is anything but straightforward. It requires considerable effort and reflection. Orona reports that 'In the beginning, I literally sat for days on end with the transcribed interviews spread out before me, absorbing them into my consciousness and letting them "float" about' (1990: 1249). She wrote memos, talked about them with friends, and explored any ideas that came to her.

One of the strengths of this form of grounded theory is that it relies on hunches and intuition, or creativity, nuance and detail (Orona 1990). The process is not linear or clear. Rather, it is often confusing, frustrating and somewhat chaotic. This is both its weakness and its strength. It leads to new ways of understanding as new ideas are put together or participants' interpretations are seen in new light. However, it is also difficult, time-consuming and demanding of energy.

The process of 'constant comparison' is one of the central methods utilised by grounded theorists in developing and identifying codes. Strauss and Corbin describe the process of constant comparison as integral to the coding process: 'As an incident is noted, it should be compared against other incidents for similarities and differences' (1990: 9). Comparisons allow data to be grouped and differentiated, as categories are identified and various pieces of data are grouped together. Through the comparative process, events that at first seemed entirely unrelated may be grouped together as different types of the same category, or events that seemed similar may be categorised differently. For example, one participant's discussion of 'living for the moment' at first seemed quite unrelated to another participant's discussion of his plans to buy a house. However, as temporality was explored as a possible category, these events were compared and identified as different aspects of the same category.

Codes have properties, and these properties have dimensions (Strauss & Corbin 1990). For example, the code 'temporality' has the properties of how people feel about the future and how they feel about the present. How people feel about the future varies along a dimension. Some despaired because of the loss of their future, others were more philosophical about the uncertain nature of the future, and others were confident of a long future. Exploring the properties and dimensions of a code can lead to the code being broken into two separate codes, or it might lead to its being amalgamated with a similar code.

Varying the units of analysis can be an important strategy during open coding. Strauss and Corbin (1990) suggest experimenting with coding lines, sentences, paragraphs and whole documents. In my own research I moved between coding lines, paragraphs, interactional events, narratives about episodes, and the structure of the interview as a whole. Printing out interview transcripts with very wide margins, preferably in landscape orientation, makes this sort of coding much easier.

The next step in coding is described as *axial coding* by Strauss and Corbin. Axial coding involves 'specifying a category (phenomenon) in terms of the conditions that give rise to it; the context (its specific set of properties) in which it is embedded; the action/interactional strategies by which it is handled, managed, carried out; and the consequences of those strategies' (1990: 97). The aim of axial coding is to integrate codes around the axes of central categories. Orona describes the transition to axial coding, saying that there came a point where she 'felt' that she had to stop reading the transcripts of interviews with participants and instead read all her own notes and memos carefully: 'For several days, I sat wading through the notes and placing them into what I felt were the major categories, which by then, had been abstracted to a higher level. Thus "silent partner", "helper", and "neighbours" had been abstracted to the level of *social relations*' (Orona 1990: 1249). She finally identified four major themes: social relations, reciprocity, moral obligation and temporality.

There is some debate among grounded theorists about the nature and value of axial coding. Strauss and Corbin (1990) argue for the value of axial coding, whereas Glaser (1978) argues that it is a process that restricts the inductive, or grounded, nature of theory building. According to the formalised method of axial coding developed by Strauss and Corbin (1990), among others, axial coding should focus on the four dimensions of context, strategy, processes and consequences. This focus on dimensions suggests a particular way of constructing data analysis that focuses the coding process on the relationship of codes to the analytic 'whole' (Schatzman 1991). The danger, of course, is that in constructing 'dimensions' the analyst may decide to focus on issues related to his or her interests rather than issues that concern the participants. In her review of this debate, Kendall (1999) describes how her data analysis became misdirected in precisely this way and developed serious problems as a consequence. Kendall's problems appear to have arisen as a consequence of beginning axial coding too early in her analysis rather than as a product of the specific methods of axial coding itself. Whichever approach is taken, Kendall's review of the issues demonstrates that the most important advice for the qualitative data analyst is to 'not become wedded too early to what looks obvious' as central categories or themes of the research (1999: 753).

In my study of people living with HIV/AIDS, the central theme of temporality was coded axially as I identified other codes associated with the various types of temporal orientations. That is to say, people who were confident about the future tended to be healthy, have good networks of friends, believed that medicine would solve the problems of HIV, and were making decisions in their lives based on this confidence in the future. On the other hand, people who despaired about the future tended to have experienced illness, were socially isolated, felt that medicine did not have the answers to HIV/AIDS, and found it difficult to plan their lives very far into the future.

Finally, *selective coding* (Strauss & Corbin 1990) or *theoretical coding* (Glaser 1978) involves the identification of the core category or story around which the analysis focuses. Crisp reports that in his analysis 'More selective coding occurred later when major themes emerged . . . [and after they were identified] core categories were repeatedly verified or revised after re-checking the transcribed interview data, and after asking the respondents whether they accepted (in everyday language) these accounts of themselves' (2000: 358).

In my own analysis of stories of living with HIV/AIDS, the core category was 'temporality' (Ezzy 2000a). I identified three different temporal orientations: some people confidently expected a normal lifetime; other people expected a short life, and were angry or depressed about this; and a third group were uncertain how long they would live, but decided to enjoy what time they had left. These temporal orientations were linked to a variety of other codes, including whether people felt in control of their life, whether they were religious, and whether their values were self-centred or communally oriented. In other words, the code 'temporality' provided the central code around which all the other codes were fitted. 'Temporality' also provided the central 'story' of my research report and of the theory that I developed to account for the different ways in which people with HIV/AIDS respond to their diagnosis.

Coding finishes when the researcher is satisfied that the theory is saturated. Morrow and Smith explain that in their analysis 'Codes and categories were sorted, compared, and contrasted until saturated—that is, until analysis produced no new codes or categories and when all of the data were accounted for in the core categories of the grounded theory paradigm model' (1995: 26). Note that saturation refers to the relationship between the codes and the emerging theory. It will always be possible to discover new information in the data, but saturation is achieved when the coding that has already been completed adequately supports and fills out the emerging theory.

Coding in grounded theory and thematic analysis

- Open coding:
  - Explore the data.
  - Identify the units of analysis.
  - Code for meanings, feelings, actions.
  - Make metaphors for data.
  - Experiment with codes.
  - Compare and contrast events, actions and feelings.
  - Break codes into subcategories.
  - Intergrate codes into more inclusive codes.
  - Identify the properties of codes.
- Axial coding:
  - Explore the codes.
  - Examine the relationships between codes.
  - Specify the conditions associated with a code.
  - Review data to confirm associations and new codes.
  - Compare codes with preexisting theory.
- Selective coding:
  - Identify the core code or central story in the analysis.
  - Examine the relationship between the core code and other codes.
  - Compare coding scheme with preexisting theory.

A sophisticated approach to coding during grounded theory mixes both inductive and deductive methods. Codes do not emerge from the data uninfluenced by preexisting theory. As argued in Chapter 1, the process of theory building involves an ongoing dialogue between data and theory. It is, however, very difficult to balance the emergent nature of codes in grounded theory against the influence of preexisting theory. Glaser observes that in grounded theory 'we do not have to discover all new categories nor ignore all categories in the literature that might apply in order to generate a grounded theory. The task is, rather, to develop an emergent fit between the data and a preexistent category that might work' (1978: 148). The process of developing an 'emergent fit' involves negotiating between categories that emerge through data analysis and knowledge of categorical schemes utilised in relevant literature and theory. The aim is to avoid the knowledge of existing theory's forcing the analysis of the data into these preexisting categories. Through a process of comparison of emergent categories with preexisting categories, new and more sophisticated understanding of the experience can be developed. Emergent codes may be named so as to be consistent with preexisting theory. However, as existing theory is integrated in the constant comparative process utilised by grounded theory, as Wuest observes, this process 'more often results in modifying and building the emerging theory such that it fits both the new data and the relevant concepts from the existing theory' (2000: 55).

In my study of people living with HIV/AIDS, the emergent category of temporality resonated with a number of existing studies that examined the temporal nature of chronic illness (Frank 1995; Davies 1997). In my final report (Ezzy 2000a), these preexisting conceptual frameworks were explicitly integrated with my own emergent theory of the role of temporality in shaping people's understanding of living with HIV/AIDS. My data were coded inductively, and as I coded I included preexisting theory as part of the constant comparative process. The research report, therefore, becomes part of an ongoing intentional dialogue about how to understand the different ways that people experience and live with HIV/AIDS.

Coding is the process of disassembling and reassembling the data. Data are disassembled when they are broken apart into lines, paragraphs or sections. These fragments are then rearranged, through coding, to produce a new understanding that explores similarities, and differences, across a number of different cases. The early part of the coding process should be confusing, with a mass of apparently unrelated material. However, as coding progresses and themes emerge, the analysis becomes more organised and structured. Careful coding allows the researcher to move beyond preexisting theory to 'hear' new interpretations and understandings present in the data.

Narrative analysis

In contrast to the qualitative sociology, mainstream academic psychology has rarely examined the person as a whole. Statistics disaggregate the individual into measurable attributes. Similarly, the traditions of grounded theory and thematic analysis, through the use of cross-case comparisons, tend to disaggregate individuals, focusing on codes and categories rather than people as the units of analysis. In contrast, narrative analysis refers to the whole of a person's account. The parts of the story become significant only as they are placed within the context of the whole narrative.

The emphasis on whole people and whole narratives represents a radical change of focus. First, it emphasises that the nature of an event or belief is not to be found in the event or belief itself, but in the relationship of the event or belief to a broader interpretive framework or narrative. This places 'purpose' at the forefront of interpretation (Freeman 1984). If a researcher wants to understand the meaning of something, he or she must locate the event or belief in a broader narrative that defines its purpose, and therefore its significance. Narrative analysis identifies the broader interpretive framework that people utilise to turn meaningless events into meaningful episodes that are part of a story leading out of the past and into the future.

Plot is one of the central characteristics of a story. Plot is a literary term for the structure of a narrative, derived from Aristotle's *Poetics* (Martin 1986). Narrative theory applies this literary analysis of plots to the study of action, arguing that lives are narrated in the same way as literary texts (Ricoeur 1984). A succession of apparently unrelated events are configured into a whole, a story with meaning, by the plot of a story. Plots explain the point, or purpose, of the events discussed (Ricoeur 1985). 'A fundamental way we create sense is by shaping the "one thing after another" character of on-going action into a coherent narrative structure with a beginning, middle and end' (Mattingly 1994: 812).

Second, the emphasis on narrative embraces a situated relativity and points to the 'in-process' nature of interpretations. Plots are not fixed by the events they describe, but are situated constructions, or acts of reading (Ricoeur 1984). Between the poles of objectivism and relativism, narrative analysis embraces the situated and continually transforming nature of interpretations and self-understanding: 'Ricoeur . . . understands the construction of narrative identity as a process that is constantly open to review. As such, it is the poetic resolution to the hermeneutic circle' (Joy 1993: 296). We all tell stories about our lives, but these stories are always open-ended. History and identity are not fixed constructs, but neither are they completely flexible and malleable. Rather, they are somewhat stable, but continually reinterpreted as we have new experiences and tell new stories about ourselves, our past, and the world around us.

Stevens and Doerr (1997) provide an excellent example of the use of narrative theory to examine the response of women to being informed of a diagnosis with HIV. Drawing on long interviews with 38 HIV-positive women, they identified sections of the transcribed interviews that reported the women's responses to their diagnosis. Their methodology is summarised in the text box below.

One narrative analysis method: Stevens and Doerr's study of HIV narratives

1. Identify the story to be examined—in this case, the participant's account of being told she had HIV.
2. Analyse the context and content of each story, particularly focusing on understandings and feelings.
3. Examine how the women described the consequences and aftermath of the diagnosis.
4. Compare and contrast the stories. Search for similarities and differences in the structure of the story plots.
5. Examine the effects of background variables such as gender, age, health status, and time since diagnosis, to see whether these are related to earlier identified patterns.
6. Examine the transcripts for sections that illustrate the types of stories identified.

(Summarised from Stevens & Doerr 1997.)

Stevens and Doerr (1997) identify three types of narratives. *Epiphany* narratives described the HIV diagnosis as a revelatory event through which the women found a new meaning to their life, producing major changes to the way they lived. *Confirmation* narratives described the HIV diagnosis as a discovery of something the women already suspected, and as such it did not change their lives significantly. These narratives tended to be emotionally muted, with a tone of resignation. Finally, *calamitous* narratives described the event of diagnosis as a shock in which the women felt they had been given a death sentence, responding with fear, anguish and intense emotions. The trauma of the diagnosis violently disrupted their previous self-narratives and took these women by surprise. These three narrative types are different ways of plotting an HIV diagnosis. They link the event of an HIV diagnosis into a series of episodes, past and future, that give it meaning and significance. The responses are not, however, fixed. It is possible, for example, for a calamitous narrative to be replaced with an epiphany narrative due to some other experience.

The calamitous narrative type is well illustrated by an interview conducted with a woman with HIV as part of a study of people living with HIV/AIDS in Australia conducted at the National Centre in HIV Social Research at La Trobe University (McDonald et al. 1998; Ezzy 2000a). This selection illustrates the nature of the narratives Stevens and Doerr describe. 'Sarah' was 36 years old when she was interviewed. She was married to 'Matt' and worked part-time. She was infected with HIV about ten years ago, when she was 26 years old, prior to her relationship with Matt. However, she did not find out she had HIV until about a year before the interview:

> I was tired and run down and da da da da, and went off to the doctor and said look I think I might be pregnant. He said the pregnancy test is negative but we'll do a blood test to make sure. I said fine. I said look while you're at it, a guy I was seeing died last year, could you run an HIV test. Pregnancy test came back negative and the HIV test came back positive. So, I had been telephoned at work, told by the doctor over the phone telling me the result had come back positive but it could be a mistake, you'd better ring your husband because he'll probably have it if you do have it, and you'd better get in here today. So, I had to ring Matt. And he's a plumber, he's at work, and I'm saying you've got to come with me to the doctor's today. What is it—I can't come today. And I had to say, you know, the AIDS test has come back positive. It couldn't have. So, we both went down to the doctor's. I'm crying, Matt's just in shock. We're sitting at the doctor's. The doctor said oh well this is my first case, I don't know what to say to you. There's really no treatment. It will be a very short life span. There's no way known you can have children. You're looking pretty good at the moment but you've had it off this guy for as long as you think you had, you won't be . . . I was the doctor's first patient. He couldn't understand that people, in a wealthy middle-class suburb get HIV. People don't get it from this area. Particularly heterosexual women. So, he just couldn't cope. They rushed through Matt's blood test. And his blood test came back negative. That often it is the case that the husband will be negative da, de, da. So that was sort of the initial sort of shock.

This narrative links a past (a previous relationship) with a social location (white heterosexual woman) and the response of others (the doctor's terrifying prognosis) to explain the trauma and shock of this woman's diagnosis with HIV. There are a variety of treatments for HIV/AIDS currently available, although they do not guarantee a healthy life. The doctor's incorrect information fed into a plot of the events that described the movement from a good life, through the trauma of diagnosis, to an anticipated difficult life. The event of diagnosis takes on meaning as a consequence of its placement in a story about this woman's life. The plot of her story is of HIV as a calamity. The events of her life are made sense of—are interpreted—within this broader narrative frame.

Narrative analysis contains a very broad range of methodologies for identifying narrative structure, and Stevens and Doerr's approach is only one among many. For example, Bamberg's (1997) edited collection contains a wide selection of narrative analysis methodologies, including a statistical cognitivist approach to narrative, an ethnomethodological conversation analysis, a functionalist linguistic study, a cross-cultural interpretive approach and a life span study. Each of these studies utilises different methodologies: some statistical, some metaphoric, some interpretive, they also draw on different theoretical paradigms, from psychological cognitivism, through linguistic theory, to hermeneutics. Riessman (1993) also provides a useful overview of several narrative analysis methods. In this short introduction I have attempted only to describe two approaches that are widely utilised in qualitative social research.

For qualitative social researchers, one of the strengths of narrative analysis is that it provides a constructive way of doing social research that engages with, rather than denies, the epistemological, ontological and methodological issues raised by contemporary social theory. Narrative analysis, as it is typically utilised in social research, draws on the hermeneutic theory of philosophers and moral theorists such as Ricoeur (1984, 1985, 1988), Taylor (1989), MacIntyre (1995) and others (see the discussion of hermeneutics in Chapter 1). The implications for qualitative methods have been explored by a number of authors, such as Polkinghorne (1988), Bruner (1990) and Riessman (1993). Some feminist researchers have similarly drawn on narrative analysis as part of a feminist response to the crisis of legitimation and representation (Personal Narratives Group 1989; Chase 1996; Richardson 1997). Bell's study of women with cancer provides an excellent illustration of this link between a sophisticated theory and the practice of narrative analysis:

> Sociological theorists are questioning the possibility of producing accurate knowledge about social life as well as how to account for the ways knowers produce knowledge: What constitutes knowledge? What constitutes a subject? What constitutes action, agency, power, or resistance? *Narrative analysis is a particularly strong way of addressing these questions* (Bell, S. 1999: 347, emphasis added).

Susan Bell (1999) utilises narrative analysis in her study of women with cancer as a consequence of their mothers' exposure to DES, a drug prescribed to prevent miscarriage. She reports that at first she began her study by trying to distance herself from the women she was interviewing. She strove for 'objectivity'. Bell did not tell her participants about her own life or commitments, and strove to select women who would not know her. However, as she become more involved in her study she become uncomfortable about the attempt to distance herself from her participants, objectifying them as objects of scientific inquiry. Influenced by feminist theory and narrative analysis, she began to be more open about her own commitments and experiences with her subjects. Her interviews became more conversational and reciprocal.

Bell's methodology differs from Stevens and Doerr's in that Bell is *less* concerned with identifying the overall plot of the narrative through an examination of *what* is said. Rather, Bell focuses on *how* the story is told. She examines narrative techniques such as the use of repetition, metaphors, phrasing, and the imagery of the story. Rather than providing cross-case comparisons, Bell examines two specific narratives in detail. Bell uses her analysis to show how the narratives of the two women she describes are integrated with broader cultural narratives (see text box, p. 100).

Narrative analysis is attractive to Susan Bell for two reasons. First, narrative analysis explicitly addresses the role of the interviewer in the construction of interview responses: 'In my interpretation of Molly's and Deborah's experiences I explore how my social position helped to construct the interview context, the production of narratives about their experiences, and my interpretation of the contexts and narratives' (Bell, S. 1999: 354). Contemporary research on long interviews has highlighted that interviews are not places where an interviewer goes and collects accounts that were preexisting in the participant's head. Rather, interviews are places where meanings, interpretations and narratives are co-constructed (Holstein & Gubrium 1995). To try to be objective, to try to avoid influencing the interview, is fruitless. Rather, the researcher should be explicit about his or her role in the interview process. Narrative analysis facilitates precisely this explicit analysis of the role of the interviewer in the construction of the interview narrative.

One narrative analysis method: Bell's study of cancer narratives

1. Identify narrative segments in the interview transcripts.
2. Examine word choice, phrasing, imagery and structure of clauses.
3. Focus on the telling of the story: how do people explain what they did, or what happened?
4. Examine how the stories relate to each other.
5. Look for connections between the personal accounts and broader cultural and political processes.
6. Locate yourself, as the researcher in the analysis and the construction of the stories.

(Summarised from Bell, S. 1999.)

Narrative analysis does not attempt to identify the one true interpretation of participants' stories. Rather, the goal is to identify the cultural and social context that facilitates the everyday practice of telling stories about oneself and one's world: 'Understanding the meaning and significance of a story requires understanding how it is communicated within or against specific cultural discourses and through specific narrative strategies and linguistic practices' (Chase 1996: 55). Narrative theory explicitly engages with the complexity of the world and the finite nature of human understanding. Human action is too complex to ever discover a final set of laws to describe it. Humans are situated, and can never know everything. As Josselson puts it: 'narratives are not records of facts, of how things actually were, but of a meaning-making system that makes sense out of the chaotic mass of perceptions and experiences of a life' (1995: 33).

Second, narrative analysis allows Bell to connect the narratives of individual women to the more general political context: 'Their narratives display the ways these women connect their individual life experiences to changing social and structural conditions in the context of the women's health movement' (Bell, S. 1999: 353). Narrative analysis allows the researcher to be explicit about the political and cultural location of both the narratives of participants and the researcher. This is precisely the point of Mills' (1959) argument, that social researchers need to grasp the link between sociopolitical processes and individual biography. Narratives exist at a variety of 'levels'. Personal narratives told in fleeting encounters such as interviews contain, represent and misrepresent narratives that an individual may hold for a considerable time, and narratives that broader sections of a community may share and may be embedded in more general cultural processes. Bell summarises her research, pointing to how her analysis links precisely these dimensions:

> My interpretations of the interview narratives show how two DES cancer daughters' perceptions and interpretations are mediated through the cultures surrounding them, how they live within and in tension with systems of domination, how their individual biographies are connected to the structural conditions in which they originate, and how their narratives are jointly produced by researcher and subject. These interpretations show how narrative analysis can demonstrate and explain the production of knowledge (Bell, S. 1999: 385).

Narrative analysis refers to a wide range of analytic methodologies. I have illustrated the practice of two of these in this section. On the one hand, Stevens and Doerr's methodology focuses more on the structure of the story, on *what* is said. The methodology they utilise is similar to, and expands on, the analytic strategies of grounded theory and thematic analysis. A side range of narrative studies have utilised similar methodologies (Gergen 1988; Bruner 1990; Mattingly 1994; Frank 1995). On the other hand, narrative analysis, as conducted by Bell, shifts the focus of the research from *what* participants say to *how* they tell their stories. This involves 'attending to the cultural, linguistic, and interactional contexts and processes of storytelling' (Chase 1995: x). This concern with broader cultural and political context is shared by cultural studies and is discussed in the next section.

Cultural studies and semiotics

> Postmoderns subvert the authority of modernist metatheory with a rhetorical conception of science . . . They do so by focusing on

101

the *how* rather than the *what* of knowledge, its poetic and political enablements rather than its logical and empirical entailments (Brown 1991: 190).

In 1997, McGuigan reported that it 'remains difficult to see quite what cultural studies amounts to methodologically' (1997: 1). This is because cultural studies is both eclectic, drawing on a wide range of method from other disciplines, and diverse, with a wide variation in methodologies that makes it difficult to identify that which is common to cultural studies. In this section I focus on cultural studies research as it is relevant to the practice of qualitative data analysis. McGuigan's (1997) book provides an excellent overview of the methodologies of cultural studies more generally.

Cultural studies has recently taken a 'turn' towards qualitative methodology. Early cultural studies focused almost exclusively on the 'text' of a television program, film or writing. This textually determinist model provides no room for an examination of how audiences dialogue with the 'text', nor does it conceive of interpretations as constructed intersubjectively. However, more recent cultural studies practitioners have recognised that 'textual meanings do not reside in the texts themselves; a certain text can come to mean different things depending on the interdiscursive context in which viewers interpret it' (Ang 1996: 38).

Interpretation in cultural studies

• Data, or the text, are interpreted in the light of broader cultural and social systems.
• What is missing from the text is as important as its manifest content.
• Preexisting theory is used to interrogate and interpret data.
• Analysis is conducted to reveal the operation of power in cultural life.
• Some researchers rely on rhetoric and aesthetics to persuade readers of the authenticity of their work, largely ignoring issues of systematic observation and analysis.
• The results of data analysis are not framed as scientifically validated truth, but as historically located, subjective and relative.

Cultural studies locates the interpretation of data within an analysis of broader social and cultural processes. Influenced by structuralism, it examines not only the manifest content but also the 'deep structure' of a text, or data: 'One must pay attention to both, looking not only at classification systems, but also at what is implied, what is not spoken, what is "really meant"' (Lamont & Wuthnow 1990: 290). Another way of saying this is that a semiotic or cultural analysis of magazines, television programs and transcribed discussions about these cultural artifacts by audiences takes the researcher outside the data. It examines the relationship between the 'data' and broader social and cultural frameworks. Cultural studies tends not to call this process 'data analysis', or 'coding', but 'interpretation', or 'reading'. This interpretive emphasis contrasts with the focus on detail and nuance character-istic of thematic analysis and grounded theory. Data are not dissected so much as contextualised. This contextualisation is not found in the data, but is drawn from a more general analysis of social and cultural processes, often informed by critical theory or feminism:

> The aim of cultural studies is not a matter of dissecting 'audience activity' in ever more refined variables and categories so that we can ultimately have a complete and generalizable formal 'map' of all dimensions of 'audience activity' . . . Rather, the aim, as I see it, is to arrive at a more historicized and contextualized insight into the ways in which 'audience activity' is articulated within and by a complex set of social, political, economic and cultural forces (Ang 1996: 42).

This analytic emphasis is often linked to a strategy of data analysis, or reading, that examines both what is *not* present in the data as well as the manifest content. To put this another way: qualitative data analysis facilitates the identification of differences in inter-pretations and experience among people, events and interactions. Thematic analysis and grounded theory use codes to attune the researcher to the structure of these differences in the lives of participants. Cultural studies is also interested in these differences, but from the perspective of locating their meanings interpretively within broader social, cultural and political contexts.

For example, McKinley (1997) utilises cultural studies methodology to examine how people talk about the prime-time soap *Beverly Hills 90210*. Reflecting the influence of cultural

103

studies' move towards ethnography, McKinley's data are not the 'text' of the program itself but the 'text' of talk about the program among 36 young women, obtained during interviews and transcriptions of talk while they were watching the program. McKinley describes how young women watch and talk about *90210* as part of a process of gender enculturation. She argues that the women actively work at constructing an understanding of gendered identity as part of their talk about this television soap. Her method of data analysis, or interpretation, explicitly 'works' the relationship between the empirical data, or text, and more general theories of cultural practice and social structure. While she describes her research as an 'empirical testing of poststructuralist theory' (McKinley 1997: 5), her analytic strategy is more complex than simply analysing data using thematic or content analysis and comparing the results with preexisting theory. Rather, the preexisting theory enters into the very way that McKinley conducts her interpretation of her data:

> The [interpretive] questions became, what female identities were seen as appropriate and/or encouraged as viewers talked about *90210*? What options were hidden? And what identities were made so natural that they were accepted as real and immutable? . . . poststructuralist feminist [theory] led me to analyze the talk about females with an eye towards ways it did—or did not—perpetuate the values of patriarch and capitalism, and to ask what the role of the television text was in generating and guiding—or not guiding—this talk (McKinley 1997: 8–9).

Unlike the methods of grounded theory, cultural studies explicitly integrates theoretical questions as part of the data analysis process. This is for two reasons. First, cultural theory locates interpretations within more general cultural and social processes. Talk about *90210* among McKinley's small group of women is informed by, and representative of, processes of 'hegemonic patriarchy': 'Time and time again, I heard viewer talk working to explore identities that challenge the patriarchal definition of womanhood, then retreating to close down these alternate possibilities and reestablish a conservative status quo' (McKinley 1997: 9).

Another way of describing this analytic strategy is suggested by Barthes' (1967, 1972) distinction between three orders of signification. Drawing on Saussure, the process of signification draws an analytic distinction that differentiates signs into two component parts of *signifiers*: the physical object such as a printed word, image or person and the *signified*, which is the mental concept or word that refers to the signifier (Fiske & Hartley 1978). The words 'female identity' are the signified that refers to the signifier of actual women. The first order of signification includes self-contained references, or the manifest content. Talk about female identity in *90210* would be analysed as simply indicative of how the women understood the relevance of the program for their self-identity. Talk about female identity is taken to indicate the actual lives of women. This is the level at which much qualitative interpretation tends to operate, or at least begin. The second order of signification refers to meanings that derive from the way society values and incorporates signs into a range of cultural practices and meanings. Female identity, both as signifier and signified, in contemporary society is typically associated with passivity, heterosexuality and subservience to men. The third order of signification links these general cultural references into a 'comprehensive, cultural picture of the world, a coherent and organized view of the reality with which we are faced' (Fiske & Hartley 1978: 41). The talk about female identity is now understood as part of a more general patriarchal and capitalist society. Cultural studies is most interested in this third order of signification.

Second, cultural studies is integrally political, asking questions about power and power relations that require a more general theoretical frame. Grossberg puts this forcefully, arguing that cultural studies is 'not about interpreting or judging texts or people, but about describing how people's everyday lives are articulated by and with culture, how they are empowered and disempowered by the particular structures and forces that organize their lives' (Grossberg 1998: 67). For example, British cultural studies has been deeply influenced by Stuart Hall's (1980) argument that cultural studies is worthwhile only for its contribution to a political radicalism. From this perspective, culture is analysed in terms of its relationship to existing social inequalities linked to class, race and gender. In British cultural studies analysis focused on how the messages of culture, such as television programs or popular novels, either supported or confronted these forms of inequality. The analytic concern was not with the 'message' of the text but with the significance of these messages for broader political issues. A television program that *did not* contain any mention of gender inequalities could therefore be analysed as contributing to the on-going nature of the oppression of women. There is some debate among cultural theorists about the value of Hall's position, although even the more pragmatic approaches retain a commitment to artic-ulating the political dimensions of their research: 'The ambition of cultural studies is to develop ways of theorizing relations of culture and power that will prove capable of being utilized by relevant social agents to bring about changes within the operation of those relations of culture and power' (Bennet 1997: 52).

In America, cultural studies has mingled critical theory with pragmatism and symbolic interactionism, in a tradition of which C. Wright Mills is emblematic (Denzin 1992). Mills' (1959) argument that sociology has a responsibility to conceptualise other possible ways of organising society, while often ignored within sociology, has been taken up within cultural studies. As Calhoun puts it: 'Cultural studies seeks . . . to explore the ways in which our categories of thought reduce our freedom by occluding recognition of what could be' (1995: xiv).

While cultural theorists recognise participants as active construc-tors of their lives, in a significant way participants are determined, or overdetermined, by broader social processes. Denzin considers that '[the participant] does not understand the historical forces that shape everyday biographical life. Only the analyst understands these forces' (1997: 236). In this sense, it is impossible to analyse people's self-understandings on their own terms. In order to make sense of a text or action, these must be translated into theoretical terms. This is precisely what McKinley does in her analysis of women's talk about a television soap: 'Gathering and analyzing empirical evidence of the ways the microprocesses of hegemony play out in talk about the show have led me to conclude that such talk is implicated—for better or worse—in the reproduction of dominant notions of female identity' (McKinley 1997: 235).

Interpretation in cultural studies is often more reflective of Goffman's first two analytic strategies of metaphor and unsystem-atic observation than of his third method of systematic observation. Paul Smith observes that British cultural studies, while committed to empirical research, has tended to eschew an emphasis on systematic methods, criticising these as overly 'positivist', and instead using methods that have more in common with the aesthet-ics of literary and art criticism: 'Traditional issues of measurement and methodology have become displaced in favor of innovative, virtuoso interpretations of media texts, youth sub-cultures, popular music lyrics, etc.' (Smith, P. 1998: 10). In contrast to the more systematic ethnography of Willis (1977), cultural theorists such as Hebdige (1979) drew on a more creative and semiological approach to cultural analysis, as exemplified in his book *Subculture*. Hebdige's work draws on a variety of eclectic sources for data and aims to produce a sensitivity to the complexity of youth subculture through the use of metaphor and models. As McGuigan puts it, his work reflects a 'poststructuralist fascination with the play of signifiers and [moves] away from "experience"' (1992: 101).

The analytic method of cultural studies contains an unresolved tension between a theoretical emphasis on analytical deduction and an empiricist inductivism. Lamont and Wuthnow (1990) point out that American cultural studies has emphasised the role of observation and empirical induction, and this is linked to a rejection by some to the radical politics characteristic of British cultural studies. European cultural studies has emphasised theoretical deduction as primary in generating new theory and interpretation, and this is often linked to a more explicit commitment to engaging with the political implications of their analysis:

> Cultural studies has in general been more willing than sociology, with its strong universalising bent, to grant that knowledge may be inherently perspectival—or to put it differently, may be both limited and enabled by the knower's historical, cultural, and social access to the world, including the world of intellectual traditions—and more eager to explore the links between knowledge and social domination (Long, 1997: 15).

Cultural studies challenges the naive inductivist empiricism of some grounded theorists. If all interpretation is from a perspective, then it is pointless to pretend that preexisting theory, or the value commitments of the researcher, have not shaped the research process. This does not make empirical research irrelevant, as some critics argue. Drawing on the theory developed in Chapter 1, I argue that it is still important to engage in systematic empirical research, and that the methods of grounded theory have considerable value in assisting this process. However, cultural theorists problematise the politics of the interpretive process, asking from whose perspective, and for whose benefit, the interpretation has been conducted. This is a question that cannot be avoided if it is accepted that all interpretation is unavoidably political. These points were taken up in detail in Chapter 2. Ang summarises the implications of taking this interpretive approach in her description of the aim of research: 'It is not the search for (objective, scientific) Truth in which the research is engaged, but the construction of *interpretations*, of certain ways of understanding the world, always historically located, subjective and relative' (Ang 1996: 46). The emphasis on the historical and subjective nature of the products of research in cultural studies also leads to an emphasis on the role of the author, and researcher, in producing the research. This is discussed more fully in Chapter 6.

Compared to the sophistication of the semiotic techniques utilised to study cultural texts, cultural studies has applied surprisingly unsophisticated methods to analyse letters, transcripts of interviews and ethnographic data (Nightingale 1993). This does not just refer to the sometimes 'thin' nature of interpretations based on barely described, and often significantly attenuated, evidence and analytic methods (McEachern 1998). Early attempts at ethnography in cultural studies often also ignored the role of the researcher in the research process.

'What occurs, then, in the absence of rigorous ethnographic observation and description, when the techniques of ethnography are divorced from ethnographic process, is a co-opting of the interviewee's experience of the text by the researcher, and its use as authority for the researcher's point of view' (Nightingale 1993: 153). This point is almost exactly the same as Glaser's (1978) point about the danger of qualitative researchers forcing their data into the categories of preexisting theories. Radaway admits to the probability that her own research was shaped in this way when she suggests that 'my initial preoccupation with the empiricist claims of social science prevented me from recognizing fully that even what I took to be simple descriptions of my interviewees' self-understandings were mediated if not produced by my own conceptual constructs and ways of seeing the world' (1991: 5). As Radaway's quote suggests, to make this point does not require a return to a naive empiricism. To argue for the importance of rigorous method does not require the abandonment of the more general political and theoretical orientations of cultural studies. It does, however, require that the researcher take equally seriously the voices of participants and the researcher's own voice. This can be achieved through a combination of rigorous method and explicit engagement with more general political and theoretical issues. Radaway suggests that if she were to revisit her research, 'I would attend more closely to the nature of the relationship that evolved between the Smithton women and me by describing the interviews themselves in greater detail and including representative transcripts from them' (1991: 5).

Cultural studies reminds us that qualitative research is an interpretive process. Interpretations are always situated, historical, subjective and political. Researchers that ignore these aspects of the interpretive process will produce an analysis that falls into predictable traps. Ignoring the situated nature of research leads to claims about the generalisability of results that are less than convincing. Ignoring political dimensions of the research leads, by default, to a politics of conservatism. Cultural studies also reminds us that interpretation is as much an art as a systematic process. It is arguable that some cultural studies researchers have ignored systematic analytic procedures to their loss. However, it is equally arguable that adherence to systematic method may give some qualitative researchers a confidence that is unfounded. Qualitative researchers should aim for a balance between systematic observation, unsystematic observation, and metaphor. As with Goffman's research, the correct mixture of these methods leads to research that is both evocative, in the sense that it produces new insights, and convincing, because it rests on systematic research.

Summary reflections

> Description demands model-building and models always distort; there is no clear window on a different culture. However, the attempt to build an account sensitive to interpretive limitations may provide a powerful understanding of the phenomenon (Luhrmann 1989: 14–15).

Each of the analytic strategies described in this chapter is a way of summarising and interpreting 'data'. The aim is not to discover, finally and objectively, what is 'out there'. Rather the aim is to engage with the data as 'other', as a participant in a conversation in which the researcher also participates. This does not mean, however, that anything goes methodologically. Systematic and rigorous data analysis strategies are both better at hearing the voice of the 'other', and provide a stronger position from which to contribute to the ongoing politically imbued conversation in which we live.

Further reading

Content analysis

Kellehear, A. 1993 *The Unobtrusive Researcher*, Sydney, Allen & Unwin.

Grounded theory and thematic analysis

Charmaz, K. 1995 'Grounded theory' in J. Smith, R. Harre and L. Van Langenhove (eds) *Rethinking Methods in Psychology*, London, Sage, pp. 27–49.
Orona, C. 1990 'Temporality and identity loss due to Alzheimer's disease' *Social Science and Medicine*, vol. 30, no. 11, pp. 1247–56.
Strauss, A. and Corbin, J. 1990 Basics of *Qualitative Research*, London, Sage.

Narrative analysis

Franzosi, R. 1998 'Narrative analysis' *Annual Review of Sociology*, vol. 24, no. 1, pp. 517–55.
Josselson, R. and Leiblich, E. (eds) 1993 *The Narrative Study of Lives*, vol. 1, London, Sage.
Personal Narratives Group 1989 *Interpreting Women's Lives*, Bloomington, Indiana University Press.
Riessman, C. 1993 *Narrative Analysis*, Newbury Park, Sage.

Cultural studies

Alasuutari, P. 1995 *Researching Culture: Qualitative Method and Cultural Studies*, London, Sage.
Fiske, J. and Hartley, J. 1978 *Reading Television*, London, Routledge.
McGuigan, J. (ed.) 1997 *Cultural Methodologies*, London, Sage.

5

Computer-assisted qualitative data analysis

> Most CAQDA[S] software diminishes the amount of labour needed to organize and code ethnographic data but does not fundamentally change the process of ethnographic analysis (Dohan & Sancheq-Jankowski 1998: 9).

This chapter provides an overview of the method of computer-assisted qualitative data analysis (CAQDAS). I first review computer-assisted content analysis, which demonstrates some of the strengths and weakness of computer-assisted analysis. The questions of whether, and when, to use computer-assisted analysis are addressed next, followed by a review of the processes of coding and retrieval with CAQDAS packages. Criteria for choosing between the available packages are suggested and some issues associated with learning to use the packages reviewed. Rather than reviewing particular programs in detail—a review that would be quickly out of date—I provide a list of internet sites from which up-to-date information and demonstration versions can be obtained. The chapter closes by highlighting the potential problems and benefits of CAQDAS.

Qualitative data analysis cannot be done *by* a computer. CAQDAS software only *facilitates* the analysis. Some people wrongly assume that a computer package can conduct qualitative data analysis on its own. The word 'assisted' in the term 'computer-assisted qualitative data analysis' (CAQDAS) clearly suggests that the computer package only assists and does not actually do the data analysis. MacMillan and McLachlan make this point forcefully when they argue that 'it must be stressed that NUD*IST [a leading CAQDAS package] does not do the analysis, nor even play much part in it' (1999: 7.3). Sophisticated search procedures, such as those available in CAQDAS packages, can help the analyst discover patterns in the data, but they cannot replace the interpretive process that is required for the analysis of these patterns. CAQDAS software cannot interpret the significance of data: it merely collates data and records the work of the analyst. The identification of meaningful categories, and relationships between these categories, can be done only by the researcher. CAQDAS packages could more correctly be referred to as 'tools for data storage and retrieval rather than tools for "data analysis"' (Kelle 1997: 1.4). For the sake of consistency, I retain the CAQDAS acronym.

Computer packages that can be utilised as part of qualitative data analysis can be divided into two broad categories: generic software, and dedicated qualitative analysis software (Fielding & Lee 1998; Weitzman & Miles 1995). Generic software includes word processors, text retrievers and textbase managers. General-purpose computer software can usefully assist qualitative data analysis. Dedicated qualitative analysis software includes code-and-retrieve programs and textual mapping software. Purpose-designed CAQDAS software provides an even greater advantage over these generalist packages, and many of the problems associated with the purpose-designed packages are also problems with the generalist packages, such as the need to have all the data in electronic format. This chapter is mainly concerned with the use of code-and-retrieve programs, as these are the most commonly used and relate most directly to the task of data analysis.

Dedicated qualitative analysis software is of two types: those that code the data, and those that map the relationship between the codes. Miles and Huberman (1994) divide programs that code the data into two types: code-and-retrieve programs, and code-based theory-building programs. However, MacMillan and McLachlan (1999) argue that to describe any CAQDAS program as 'theory building' is deceptive because it gives the impression that the program actually builds theory, when it does not. To avoid creating this false impression I refer to all such programs as simply code-and-retrieve programs. As their names suggest, these programs can be thought of as sophisticated index systems. They allow data to be categorised (coded), stored, and then retrieved selectively using the codes as the criteria for selection.

The relationship of the index, or coding scheme, to the documents is similar to the relationship between internet search engines and world wide web pages. Search engines create lists of web pages in which the requested text appears. CAQDAS software creates indexes of the coded documents, in which all of the requested codes appear. The text segments relevant to these lists can be collected, printed and viewed together.

Conceptual network builders and textual mapping software allow researchers to map the relationships between codes. These programs are electronic versions of the paper-and-pencil art of drawing diagrams of the relationships between codes. Some can be connected to CAQDAS packages, so that the coding scheme can be ported between the two packages. The software allows the researcher to draw a map, where categories are represented as 'nodes' with lines indicating the type of relationship between the categories. Miles and Huberman (1994) and Bryman (2001) both provide an excellent description of the varieties of software available in this class.

Computer-assisted content analysis

Computers are best able to assist with content analysis when the unit of analysis is a word, phrase or idea that can be linked to a group of words. There are a number of programs available that can be used to conduct a content analysis of an electronic text (Weitzman & Miles 1995). At the most rudimentary level, these programs search texts to count the occurrence of predetermined words. The output of the analysis is a concordance or a list of frequencies of the distribution of words. Some programs also use dictionaries to search for related words, automatically recode words into words with the same stem, and categorise words according the various predetermined categories. Further, some programs will identify words that cluster together, or that appear in the same sentence or paragraph.

In qualitative research, content analysis rarely focuses solely on the use of specific words, but on ideas and meanings. For example, in the content analysis of textbooks discussed in Chapter 4 the units of analysis are not words but personality traits attributed to different characters in the stories (Evans & Davies 2000). If groups of words associated with particular traits could be identified it might be possible for this process to be automated. However, it is doubtful that automating such a task with a computer program would improve the efficiency of this analysis, given the significantly increased time that would be required to both obtain the texts in a computer-readable format and then to set up the program to ensure that it did not attribute traits to incorrect characters. Given the small size of the project, it is probable that attempting to automate the project would take more time than conducting it manually. However, if there were a much larger number of texts to be analysed and these were relatively easily obtainable, then the effort and time required for setting up and verifying the automation of the content analysis might be worthwhile.

Some advertisements for content analysis programs incorrectly claim that the program eliminates the subjective element in the analysis of open-ended questions. For example, the web page describing Textsmart, a content analysis program produced by SPSS, claims that by using the program the analyst obtains 'a clear, unbiased representation of her respondents' attitudes and perceptions' (Textsmart 2000). This claim, of course, ignores the earlier steps in the content analysis process in which the analyst must review a computer-generated list of key terms and then 'clean and refine this list of terms by excluding trivial terms and grouping synonyms into aliases'. These aliases are in turn clustered into categories that the analyst 'revises . . . to meet her specifications'. In other words, the subjective process of selection and specification is integral to the analysis process.

Coding of meaning cannot be completely automated. When content analyses are conducted utilising computer-assisted automated techniques, it still requires that the analyst review and verify the coding. For example, Abrahamson and Park (1994) conducted a content analysis of corporate presidents' letters to shareholders to examine variations in the disclosure of negative organisational outcomes. They describe a three-step process of coding whether a letter contained a reference to a negative organisational outcome. First, they used a computer program to create a concordance of all terms that appeared in the letters under examination. This list of terms was reviewed to identify words that might be associated with negative corporate outcomes. Second, they extracted from each presidents' letters the paragraphs in which these words appeared and manually coded whether or not the words referred to negative organisational outcomes. Because words are polyvalent, with many possible meanings, this manual step was essential to ensure that the words coded actually referred to a negative organisational outcome and not to some other aspect of organisational action. Finally, these manual codes were entered in the electronic text and a computer program was used to count the occurrence of negative organisational outcomes in each letter. This was used as a dependent variable in their analysis. Clearly, if content analysis is concerned with meaning then the automation of coding is not something that can easily be achieved through computerisation. Nonetheless, the use of computerisation probably made the process more efficient and more rigorous.

Text retrievers are programs that have extensive search capabilities—including, for example, the ability to search for words with similar meanings, or for particular patterns of words. Text retrievers do not allow the researcher to code and retrieve, rather they provide distributions of words and their clustering. As with content analysis, this can be a useful starting point for a research project, though its usefulness will depend on the analytic strategy of the project. Textbase managers provide similar searching capabilities to text retrievers, but they also facilitate the management of the data to be analysed. However, they cannot be used to code and retrieve. Both Weitzman and Miles (1995) and Fielding and Lee (1998) provide some excellent discussion and examples of these programs.

Interpretive analysis

Before the advent of computers, analysts using thematic analysis or grounded theory coded and organised their data manually:

> We first had a scissor party to cut out the individual data bits and we dumped them unceremoniously in a pile . . . we laid out sheets of paper on a large table and began scanning the data for categories of phenomena and for relationships among the categories . . . As we found similarities of units, we assembled them into piles of look-alike, feel-alike groups. We wound up with sixteen stacks, or categories, into which the data seemed to fall naturally. These sixteen categories served as our initial category set, and we assigned some initial short names to these according to our interpretation of what each seemed to be saying (Carney et al. 1997: 1).

More recently, word processors have been used to perform similar tasks. Garrett (1998), for example, describes how she electronically cut and pasted her data into different documents according to themes. Carney and associates (1997) describe a clever use of the sort function in a word processor to perform a quite complex code-and-retrieve task on their data. They use symbols at the beginning of each paragraph as codes, and they collate the paragraphs using the word processor's sort function. Many of these tasks could be automated using the macro facility available in contemporary word processors (Ryan 1993).

In quantitative statistics the benefits of computer analysis are clear, and many analyses could not be contemplated without a computer. However, in qualitative research the benefits are more ambiguous, with increased efficiency in retrieval of data balanced against the higher costs associated with different resource requirements, additional learning and formatting tasks, and limitations of the available packages.

When to use a computer package

The choices of whether to use computer-assisted analysis, which package to use, and when to use it, should all follow a simple rule: first, choose both the form of analysis, and the data to be analysed, then look to see whether a computer package is available to make the analysis of these sorts of data more efficient. The choice to use computer-assisted analysis necessarily involves a choice to use particular sorts of data, and a choice to analyse these data in particular ways.

Manual methods of data analysis allow for a much greater variety of data to be utilised than is possible with computers. CAQDAS packages are typically useful only for analysing plain text documents in electronic format. Pictures, video, music, sculptures and printed text cannot be easily analysed, although, if you have the appropriate hardware and the pictures are already in electronic format, or you have access to a scanner, some software packages do allow images to be coded and analysed. While analysis of these forms of data may be performed using existing packages, it can be very time-consuming and may require scanning, reformatting, and resource-intensive applications and hardware. The manual process of photocopying and sorting photos or newspaper articles may be much more efficient and less frustrating.

There has been considerable debate in the research literature about whether CAQDAS software 'forces' users to adopt particular analytic strategies. If the analytic strategy chosen by the researcher involves some variation on content analysis or the code-and-retrieve methodology typical of grounded theory and thematic analysis, then it is unlikely that CAQDAS software will force the researcher into a particular analytic strategy—although different packages do have significantly different emphases and, as Barry (1998) notes, there may be a higher risk of being 'forced' into a particular analytic strategy for novice researchers. However, if the analytic strategy does not primarily involve a systematic code-and-retrieve procedure, as is the case for some methods that draw on cultural studies or narrative theory, the use of CAQDAS packages is more problematic.

If the analysis involves thematic analysis or grounded theory, or another similar strategy, then Weitzman and Miles' advice is worth considering seriously: 'Code-and-retrieve programs—even the weakest of them—are a quantum leap forward from the old scissors-and-paper approach: They're more flexible, and much, much faster' (1995: 18). Manual methods for thematic or grounded theory analysis of qualitative data are not only less efficient, they are also likely to discourage all but the most determined researcher from exploring the data from many points of view that the software makes possible. Fielding and Lee report the results of a focus group study of CAQDAS package users. While users experienced significant frustrations with both learning and using the packages, they found that 'with some exceptions, the computer delivered data management benefits rather than transforming analytic practice' (Fielding & Lee, 1998: 84). The strength of CAQDAS software is the efficient and systematic management of data for code-and-retrieve forms of analysis.

However, some other analytic strategies are only marginally assisted by CAQDAS packages. For example, for discourse analysis, case studies and narrative analysis, the benefits of using a CAQDAS package are uncertain. MacMillan and McLachlan report that the CAQDAS package they used to assist a discourse analysis 'was no more helpful for us in connecting the data and methods . . . than a well-organized set of files would have been' (1999: 7.3).

Current debates in the qualitative methodological literature are not generally concerned with the adoption of computer-assisted analysis. Rather, current methodological debates focus around the twofold crisis of legitimation and representation (Denzin 1997) raised by poststructuralists, cultural theory and feminism. The traditional legitimations for qualitative data collection and analysis have been undermined alongside traditional forms of representing the findings of qualitative research. This is a particularly hostile environment for computer-assisted methods 'that are often associated with a positivist approach to data analysis' (Dohan & Sancheq-Jankowski 1998: 9). CAQDAS software has little to offer the methodological debates about the crisis of legitimation and representation, and is probably perceived as a technology that supports practitioners wanting to avoid dealing with these issues.

The term 'computer-assisted qualitative data analysis' (CAQDAS) suggests an objectivity derived from computational analysis of data. Some analysts claim that the use of a CAQDAS package will make the research method more rigorous. Kelle observes that these arguments can be utilised 'as a strategic means to convince funding boards that the proposed research endeavour will be carried out in a rigorous and scholarly way' (1997: 1.4). However, such arguments link CAQDAS packages to a positivist understanding of the research process, and raise the suspicion of qualitative practitioners who have a more interpretive approach to research drawn from symbolic interactionism or cultural studies.

Many of the assumptions and methods that are inscribed in CAQDAS software require that the researcher perform code-and-retrieve based analysis. Similarly, the training courses and manuals associated with them often draw on a positivist rhetoric to justify their method and focus on variations of thematic analysis.

The emphasis of CAQDAS packages on thematic analysis, grounded theory and code-and-retrieve forms of analysis has led Coffey, Holbrook and Atkinson (1996) to warn of the danger of CAQDAS packages encouraging a new orthodoxy in analysis. The packages appear to assume that code-and-retrieve is the only form of possible analysis. Lee and Fielding (1996) appear to misunderstand this concern. They provide a list of methods books, which are not grounded theory methods books, that are cited by research reports who also cite the CAQDAS program 'the Ethnograph'. They therefore argue that CAQDAS does not encourage grounded theory, as Coffey and her associates claim. However, Lee and Fielding fail to note that most of the methods books they list advocate a variation on code-and-retrieve analytic methods and do not engage with the crises of legitimation and representation to which Coffey and associates refer. In other words, Fielding and Lee's list of references only supports the point that CAQDAS packages require the analyst to engage in a form of code-and-retrieve procedure to analyse and interpret data: 'As a consequence, there is an increasing danger of seeing coding data segments as an analytic strategy in its own right, and of seeing such an approach as the analytic strategy of choice' (Coffey et al. 1996: 7.7).

CAQDAS packages are based on code-and-retrieve techniques of data organisation. The point, simply, is that this is not the only data organisation strategy that can be used to analyse or present qualitative data, but that CAQDAS packages sometimes make it appear as if it were the only possible strategy. The strength of CAQDAS packages is that they make codification and routinised tasks efficient. However, if these sorts of tasks are not central to the analytic process, it does not make much sense to try to use computer assistance for the analysis. Researchers, and particularly novice researchers, should not feel that code-and-retrieve is the preferred method of analysis simply because that is what is supported by computer software.

A balanced assessment of the benefits and disadvantages of CAQDAS software is not assisted by claims that 'the debate about *whether* to compute in qualitative research seems to be over . . . All researchers working in the qualitative mode will be clearly helped by some computer software' (Richards, quoted in Buston 1997: 1.2). While this may be true with respect to the use of word processors, it is not true with respect to CAQDAS packages. This sort of advice ignores the documented disadvantages of computer-assisted analysis and fails to recognise the plurality of analytic methods available to qualitative researchers, including recent innovations such as autoethnography (Ellis 1995a), ethno-drama or ethno-theatre (Coffey et al. 1996), and poetry (Richardson 1997).

There is no doubt that CAQDAS software is a more efficient, systematic method for conducting code-and-retrieve analysis with data of a particular type in research projects with particular resources. However, data analysis is not necessarily best achieved through the linear, predictable and clearly structured methods that CAQDAS packages perform so well. Rather, problem solving involves a mixture of order and chaos: 'The brain searches for the best solution to a problem through a unique combination of order and randomness that optimises the scope of that search' (Torre 1995: 186).

Reading through printed transcripts, and keeping annotated copies of these, can be a useful adjunct to utilising CAQDAS software. An informative parallel may be drawn with studies of the ability of students to find information from on-line sources compared to paper or print equivalents. Landauer reports that, in nine scientific studies that examined the ability to find answers to questions in a particular text: 'in almost all cases, users were

119

quicker and more successful using paper and print than with the electronic form' (Landauer 1996: 35). However, recalling information from a text is quite different from managing the huge amount of information that can be generated in qualitative data analysis. Trying to manage the indexing system required for a complex analysis can be very difficult, and it is this aspect of qualitative data analysis that CAQDAS software does best.

CAQDAS can require significant financial investment in software, hardware and technical support. Some researchers report considerable technical difficulties as the size of their project grows, requiring additional memory and solutions to various technical problems. This can be particularly difficult if you have limited computing resources, are unable to upgrade your computer, or have limited access to technical support. There is a disturbing note in Weitzman and Miles' text on computer programs for qualitative data analysis. They comment that the manual for NUD*IST version 3 says 'you need 3MB of RAM but, in practice NUD*IST will try to take 5MB' (Weitzman & Miles 1995: 238). Although there have been newer additions of the program, this note highlights that access to 'a computer' or even one that meets the minimal stated standards in the manual may not be enough to ensure that the program will run quickly or stably.

Not everyone has access to the software, hardware and technical support required to make the use of CAQDAS software efficient. Time may constrain the busy academic as much as economics may constrain the postgraduate student. Resources available need to be weighed against analytic strategy to decide whether the considerable investment of time and money required to utilise CAQDAS software effectively is worthwhile.

Most researchers utilise a mixture of CAQDAS software and other methods to conduct their analysis. Barry's description of her use of CAQDAS software illustrates this point:

> In my own research, I use Nudist as just one tool in my analysis armoury, as it only helps me to do part of the work of analysis. For cross-case thematic analysis I find Nudist a useful way to gather data together and then play with it. For the case study and temporal aspects of my data I am happier using a word processing package to gather data together into a holistic, narrative sequence. For theorising, and abstracting meaning from the coding I find hand-drawn diagrams and tables . . . a very useful tool (Barry 1998: 2.7).

To use or not to use a CAQDAS package?

- First choose your analytic strategy and see whether a CAQDAS package is available to assist this form of analysis.
- Identify your data. If they are not in electronic format, how difficult or expensive will it be to convert them? CAQDAS analysis of non-electronic data is of arguable benefit.
- CAQDAS packages are much more efficient for some analytic tasks, particularly code-and-retrieve.
- CAQDAS packages are not very useful adjuncts to some tasks, such as some forms of narrative analysis or semiotics.
- Do you have adequate hardware to run the program?
- Do you have time to learn to use the program?

In summary, CAQDAS software clearly makes analysis of qualitative data more efficient *if* the analytic strategy involves a variation on code-and-retrieve, the researcher has access to adequate resources, and the data are available electronically. There are a number of good reasons for choosing not to use computers to assist with analysis, particularly associated with choices to experiment with analytic strategies. However, even in this case, it should be recognised that computer assistance of data analysis is just that—assistance. In many cases it may be possible to usefully integrate computer assistance into one part of the analysis. It is up to the researcher to ensure that the choice of data and analytic method is carefully considered, rather than constrained by the requirements and limitations of available software.

Coding

Once the decision has been made to use a CAQDAS package, the researcher is confronted by the task of how to integrate traditional discussions of coding with the facilities provided by the package chosen. This section describes some general principles for coding with a CAQDAS package.

The first task that confronts a researcher beginning to use a CAQDAS package is 'introducing' the documents into the software program. This is not as straightforward as it may seem. Most require that the documents be plain text, so any formatting should be removed and the information contained in it converted to plain text. Some require that the document be in a specific format, with no more than a certain number of characters per line, or with spacing at the beginning of each line, except for speaker identifiers. Others require that you decide prior to the analysis what the unit of analysis will be (line, paragraph, turn at speaking), and separate each text segment that forms the unit of analysis with a blank line. Others provide the option of including headers that are used as guides for retrieving text. Once the text has been correctly formatted and 'introduced' the coding can begin.

Coding with CAQDAS

Familiarisation: generating an initial focus

CAQDAS software facilitates familiarisation though early coding of data, the ability to auto-code and explore these auto-coded segments, and the ease with which codes can be separated and merged.

How many codes?

The computer allows a first 'trawl' with many codes and then facilitates the reduction of these codes to a manageable number that are linked to core themes. Code reduction involves both reducing the number of codes and identifying the themes around which the remaining codes cohere.

Defining codes

Code definitions develop both from inspecting data and preexisting theory. Easy reorganisation of coding schemes means that code definitions can evolve more easily. The ability to retrieve easily all segments of text previously coded with a particular code facilitates the development of consistent codes and allows the relationships between codes to be identified more clearly.

Using a codebook

Codebooks describe the shared characteristics of the codes used in the analysis. Retrieval of segments similarly coded facilitates consistency of coding, and clear code definitions. Many programs provide audit trails of the development and changes made to codes.

(Summarised from Fielding & Lee 1998.)

Coding can begin either on paper versions of documents or using 'on-screen' facilities within a computer package. While computer packages save time in retrieving documents, they typically take more time to code a document than manual methods. The more flexible the initial coding scheme, and the more inductive the emphasis of the research, the more likely it is that time and energy will be wasted if coding on screen is begun too early. If the researcher already has a clear idea of how he or she will code the data, then it makes more sense to begin coding on screen early. I prefer to begin my analysis by reading and rereading whole transcripts or documents, making marginal annotations, and highlighting text relevant to the research questions. After initial themes have been identified, I then begin to code the data using the computer package. The point at which to begin coding using the computer package will vary depending on the research objectives and the development of the analysis process. On the one hand, if computer-based coding is initiated too early, when the coding scheme is still very uncertain, then documents that were coded early in the analysis will probably require recoding when the coding scheme becomes more developed. On the other hand, there are many advantages to coding with a CAQDAS package, such as being able to utilise the auto-coding facility described below, and to run preliminary analyses while the coding is still underway.

Coding in qualitative research involves very different processes from coding in quantitative research. Charmaz describes this clearly: 'Quantitative coding requires preconceived, logically deduced codes into which the data are placed. Qualitative coding, in contrast, means creating categories from interpretations of the data' (Charmaz 1983: 111). In quantitative statistical research, coding involves deciding whether a case fits into one of a number of mutually exclusive categories, such as male versus female, or financially stressed versus financially comfortable. In qualitative research, coding often involves assigning a code to any material that appears relevant to a particular issue. For example, during my coding of the experience of unemployment I utilised one code, 'financial issues', to cover both people who said they were financially comfortable and those who were financially distressed. While I knew early in my research that financial issues were an important factor, I had not decided prior to the research how I would analyse financial issues, as this was something that I expected to discover inductively from the data. Because of the exploratory and generic nature of qualitative codes, Kelle (1997) points out that they are not very useful if applied to a positivist attempt to test empirically the relationship between two defined variables:

> The theoretical knowledge of the qualitative research does not represent a fully coherent network of explicit propositions from which precisely formulated and empirically testable statements can be deduced. Rather it forms a loosely connected "heuristic framework" of concepts which helps the researcher to focus his or her attention on certain phenomena in the empirical field (Kelle 1997: 4.4).

Auto-coding is a procedure available in many CAQDAS packages where the program searches for the occurrence of a particular word or phrase and codes all text segments containing that word or phrase with a particular code. Auto-coding can be used as a precursor to, or to facilitate, interpretive coding. For example, when analysing my data on the experience of unemployment (Ezzy 2000b) I wondered whether people who had received a redundancy payment or package found it easier to cope with losing their job. I auto-coded on the terms 'redundancy', 'package', and 'payout'. I then went through all the selections retrieved by this auto-code, and removed the ones that did not refer to receiving a redundancy package, such as one person who talked about a birthday 'package' and another who complained about not receiving a package. I was then able to compare the experience of the people who had received a package with those who had not, and found that the people who said they had received a package were more likely to report that they coped well with the loss of their job. Using this method took no more than 20 minutes, and was much more efficient than physically reading through all the transcripts. However, I later found a reference to one participant who received a 'bundle of money' on his retrenchment, which the auto-code had not picked up. Auto-coding is most useful for coding demographic data, or responses to particular questions. It is more efficient than manual analysis because of the speed of retrieval. For an auto-code to become an analytic category it has to be *interpreted*. Using auto-coding carries the danger of missing relevant discussions that do not include the words searched. However, it has the benefit of quickly identifying and locating text that may otherwise have been overlooked.

Auto-coding is not a substitute for the interpretive coding required in qualitative data analysis. Marshall reports that some

CAQDAS users consider the term auto-coding misleading, because it encourages the impression 'that qualitative data analysis packages offer artificial intelligence' (Marshall 1999: 7). Some people expect that a CAQDAS package will know how to code. Qualitative data analysis is typically concerned with meanings, and these cannot easily be predefined by the use of particular words, and as a consequence cannot easily be auto-coded.

Buston (1997) provides a detailed description of her experience of coding with a CAQDAS package. She reports that the building of an index, or coding categories, began before the first document was introduced. A preliminary coding scheme was developed drawing on headings from the interview schedule and concepts identified in the literature review. This was entered in the coding system on the CAQDAS package. After the first document was introduced, it was read through carefully and each segment of text relevant to the research question was coded: 'New coding categories were created as new ideas and ways of looking at the issues became apparent from examining the [data] . . . the preliminary [coding scheme] expanded to around ten times its original size as the analytic process proceeded' (Buston 1997: 6.6). Buston utilised the auto-code feature to facilitate 'retrospective' coding. When a new issue was identified during the analysis, documents already processed were searched using the auto-code feature and all segments identified were coded with the newly identified code. Her coding scheme evolved both through the development of sub-categories for codes that contained a great deal of variation and through the amalgamation of codes that were too fine-grained.

The use of CAQDAS packages often leads to the coding problem of *too many codes*. Fielding and Lee (1998) report an interview with a research team that abandoned CAQDAS software because the combination of the different perspectives of team members, and attention to detail facilitated by the package, led to a proliferation of codes that they found too difficult to resolve. It may be possible to overcome this sort of problem by ensuring that coding the data is done concurrently with reviewing the coding scheme. The analytic work of thinking about the evolving coding scheme should not be left until all the coding has been completed. Rather, the two tasks should be done concurrently.

There is a temptation while coding in a CAQDAS package, and in manual coding for that matter, to routinise the coding procedure so that it loses its analytic significance. I have worked coding data where I sat for too long in front of a computer clicking buttons and typing codes. Coding became something that I did almost as a reflex action without thinking very much about the implications of the text for the codes I was applying. Coding became a burdensome task rather than an invitation to interpretation. Time pressures can exacerbate this tendency. Taking regular breaks while coding can be useful both as an opportunity to reflect on the coding process and as a way of avoiding repetitive strain injury! It is probably also important to include the regular writing of memos as part of the coding process. Memos, as noted in Chapter 4, encourage contextualisation of data and analytic reflections that link the coding process to the research questions. I have also found activities that encourage reflection, such as walking, to be an important part of my coding and data analysis work. Like the writing of memos, these activities provide time to reflect and to play with ideas, and encourage the aesthetic and reflective side of the analysis process that cannot be systematised.

Some packages offer the potential to integrate the use of memos in the analysis process. This can be particularly useful if the package also allows the memos to be searched and selectively retrieved in a similar manner to data selection and retrieval. Buston reports that her memos written within the CAQDAS package were 'invaluable when it came to the later stages of the project' (Buston 1997: 8.5). They facilitated the consolidation of ideas, the identification of interesting cases, reminded of the context of text segments, and provided embryonic theory.

There are, however, several costs associated with integrating memos. Integrating memos in the data analysis software increases the dependence of the researcher on the computer. It also increases the amount of storage space required on the computer and will slow processing times, potentially limiting the amount of data that can be analysed, as is the case with NVivo (Richards 1999). Integrating the writing of memos in the data analysis software may bring the memos 'closer' to the analysis process. Writing memos separately in a word processing package, or by hand, may reduce the overall integration of the analysis with the data, but it may 'bolster a sociological imagination that extends beyond the parameters of a particular software package' (Dohan & Sancheq-Janowski 1998: 3).

Coding in qualitative data analysis is not a mechanical process that can be automated. It is an interpretive task that requires intellectual effort. The researcher must do the thinking, interpreting and conceptualisation of codes. Whether this is done 'on screen' or on paper depends on a variety of issues, including available resources, analytic strategy and personal preference.

Coding finishes for a number of reasons, some better than others. There is no 'final' interpretation, no one right way of making sense of what a document, experience or event 'means'. As a consequence, it is possible to continue coding forever, or at least for a very long time. Considerations of time, money and flagging interest often restrict the length of coding. This is not always a bad thing, as continued exploration of new ideas has to stop somewhere. Time and money restrictions can, however, lead to superficial analyses, if there is not enough 'depth' in the coding. 'Depth' is a notoriously vague criterion, and bears some similarities to 'theoretical saturation' (see Chapter 4). The criterion for stopping coding can be better thought of as related to whether the coding has provided enough insight or new ideas to allow the researcher to make a contribution to the ongoing dialogue about the issue under examination. Coding stops when the information produced, the 'findings', will interest other people also concerned with the research topic. If the research topic is relatively new, such as living with hepatitis C, and the audience is not interested in theoretical abstractions (an audience of policy makers for example), then a relatively short time coding data may be sufficient to produce interesting, relevant and useful results. However, if the issue has been carefully researched previously, such as the experience of unemployed people, and the audience is interested in theoretical abstractions, as required by academic journals, then coding of sufficient depth may take considerably longer.

Retrieval

Ease of retrieval is one of the major advantages of CAQDAS software. When writing up my data on job loss, I wanted to summarise the types of job losses that occurred in my sample. I had coded my data with the category 'job loss event'. In a matter of seconds I was able to retrieve all segments of text that had been coded 'job loss event', collated into one document. I then printed these out and read through them in order to summarise the different types of job losses I had studied. To do this by hand would have been an arduous task.

Selective retrieval is another of the major benefits of CAQDAS software. Documents, or coded segments, can be retrieved according to selective criteria, such as the gender of interviewees, their age or other characteristics. For example, in my research on responses to job loss I identified two main types of response to job loss: tragic narratives, and heroic narratives (Ezzy 2000a). I also identified a number of different factors that shaped the response to job loss, such as the length of notice, financial resources and plans for the future. Using selective retrieval I was able to collate all references to these factors, sorted by the type of job loss with which they were associated. I obtained a printout, for example, of all references to 'plans for the future' for people whom I had categorised as having a tragic response to their job loss. I was then able to summarise the type of plans for the future characteristic of people with a tragic job loss narrative. To do this by hand on manually coded data would have taken considerably more effort and time.

It should be underlined that selective retrieval is not a form of hypothesis testing (Kelle 1997; Fielding & Lee 1998). The different nature of coding in qualitative research, and the different logic of sample selection, means that the co-occurrence of codes by itself does not indicate anything. Rather, the meaning of the retrieved text is interpreted by the researcher, as part of the analysis process. Some packages provide the possibility of performing statistical tests on the co-occurrence of codes, or of exporting data to SPSS. Mason (1996) suggests that this can lead to a form of categorical analysis where data are treated as variables and subjected to quantitative analysis. However, this form of analysis presumes a positivist analytic framework and coding based on mutually exclusive categories, and this is typically not the case in qualitative analysis.

While transcription and the initial coding using CAQDAS software can be laborious, once people begin to use the retrieval functions of the software they often report that the analytic process becomes more creative and playful. The ease of performing a selective retrieval of codes allows researchers to explore ideas and experiment with the data to see whether patterns are in these data that might be suggested by preexisting theory or analytic hunches.

CAQDAS packages make the task of managing data more efficient and less overwhelming. They substantially increase the amount of data that can be managed and analysed. Buston reports that using a CAQDAS package 'allowed me to play around with the data however I wished, print-outs were always available quickly for me to scribble thoughts on, facilitating the development of theory in a highly organised and systematic way (I doubt manual methods would have enabled such a degree of flexibility)' (1997: 10.5).

Choosing a CAQDAS program

Different CAQDAS packages have an elective affinity to, or are more supportive of, different theoretical orientations. There are a number of different types of code-and-retrieve analytic methods that reflect different theoretical frameworks. Content analysis and grounded theory, for example, both use code-and-retrieve methods of analysis, but one typically utilises deductive theory and the other inductive theory generation. Some software packages are more supportive of one method than others. Mangabeira (1996) suggests that software developers and marketers are likely to argue that their package is neutral or not imbued with a particular methodology because this will improve sales. While the different packages are quite flexible, and are unlikely to 'force' the analyst to adopt a particular style of code-and-retrieve analysis, they do have significant differences in emphasis. Fielding and Lee (1998) argue that users will abandon a particular package if it does not suit their methodology, rather than be 'forced' to adopt a particular methodology. Nonetheless, CAQDAS programs can still exert a constraining influence on the data analysis technique, particularly for novice qualitative researchers.

'A key question is what versions of social science reasoning get built into the software. Which research methodology is being sold?' (Mangabeira 1996: 200). This should not be read as a sort of technological determinism. Clearly, the social and cultural practices associated with the package are integral in shaping what people think can, cannot and should be done with the package. One way of assessing the sort of analysis best suited to the software is to examine the manuals to see what sort of analysis is illustrated in them and what sort of methodological references are suggested. It may also be valuable to conduct a search of research databases such as the *Social Science Citation Index*, to see what sorts of studies cite the use of the program.

Researchers who have used CAQDAS packages and conducted similar research, or used a similar methodology, may also be useful sources of information. Ongoing support can be an important reason for choosing a particular package. Problems in using the package can be more easily resolved if there are other users nearby. Many packages have email lists, specific to their software package, where problems can be discussed and advice sought. These can be found through the program-specific web sites listed in the text box on p. 131.

The nature of the differences that exist between the various programs is suggested by Barry's (1998) comparison of NUD*IST and Atlas/ti, two leading CAQDAS programs that can perform code-and-retrieve functions, and that provide for memos and sophisticated searching. Her analysis is not entirely accurate, because she incorrectly claims that Atlas/ti does not have a sophisticated search facility, when it clearly does. Nonetheless, her comparison of other features is insightful:

> [Atlas/ti] has a more complex inter-connected, hypertext structure and it is more intuitive and easier to learn. Nudist has a more sequential, linear structure. It also has a clumsier interface, is less intuitive and less easy to learn . . . Nudist represents a sophisticated coding and theory building package and Atlas/ti is more of a hypertext package. Atlas/ti operates in a more visual and spatial medium with data and software functions organised in pictorial form, while Nudist operation is predominantly verbal (Barry 1998: 6.2).

The best way to decide which program to use is to experiment with a demonstration version. One of the most useful sites is the CAQDAS networking project in the United Kingdom, which provides links to downloads of demonstration versions, general and program-specific email discussion lists, and other relevant web sites: (<http://caqdas.soc.surrey.ac.uk>). Comparisons of the programs provided in books, such as that of Weitzman and Miles (1995), are rapidly out of date because new versions of programs come out relatively frequently. More up-to-date comparisons might be found, for example, at web sites such as that of Susan Friese <http://www.quarc.de>, who provides a detailed comparison of Atlas/ti, Ethnograph, QSR NUD*IST, and WinMax 97.

Learning to use a CAQDAS package

Learning to use a computer package to assist with qualitative data analysis requires learning a number of skills that you may or may not already possess. Dohan and Sancheq-Janowski point out that researchers considering utilising a CAQDAS package 'must scale several learning curves (which programs are available, what are the basics of seemingly appropriate ones, what is the actual operation

---

CAQDAS programs on the World Wide Web

AQUAD	www.uni-tuebingen.de/uni/sei/ a-ppsy/aquad/aquad.htm
Atlas/ti	www.atlasti.de
Code-a-Text	www.banxia.com
HyperRESEARCH	www.researchware.com
KWALITAN	www.kun.nl/methoden/kwalitan
QSR NUD*IST	www.qsr.com.au
QSR NVivo	www.qsr.com.au
The Ethnograph	www.QualisResearch.com
WinMax	www.winmax.de
Scolari (distributor)	www.scolari.com

---

of the selected one) and then shape their data and analysis to the requirements of the chosen software package' (Dohan & Sancheq-Janowski 1998: 9).

First, the person needs to learn to use a computer competently. For example, when a CAQDAS package is used, all the investment is in the electronic file that is created. It is absolutely essential, therefore, that users be skilled in how to back up their files routinely. Second, the use of CAQDAS requires competency in qualitative theory and method in general.

Third, the person requires competency in the detail of how to use the specific CAQDAS package. Many of the packages provide a large number of features that require considerable time to learn. The investment of time required should not be underestimated. As an indicator, some of the basic training courses last five days. To attain basic proficiency in a package probably requires at least a few weeks of dedicated use. Researchers should expect to use basic functions first, early in the analysis, and only later to move on to using the more sophisticated functions. There is evidence that many users of CAQDAS packages never utilise the more complex procedures that are available, restricting their use of the packages to straightforward code-and-retrievel tasks (Kelle 1997).

Training courses are offered by various institutions in the use of some computer packages designed to assist qualitative data. Short courses in general suffer from the problem that they are attended by people with a wide range of experience. These courses typically train people in the use of the program, and not in qualitative method in general. It is often the case that people attending these courses need to learn a number of skills, not just the use of the software package.

Potential problems with CAQDAS

Some problems researchers anticipated with CAQDAS-assisted analysis are genuine, others are not. A balanced assessment of CAQDAS software should recognise both its strengths and weaknesses. On the one hand, overblown fears, fuelled by technophobia, are not good justifications for avoiding the use of analytic tools that may improve the efficiency and depth of the analysis. On the other hand, genuine problems and documented shortcomings need to be clearly identified, and their potential impact taken into account. Lee and Fielding (1991) suggest that CAQDAS has a number of genuine dangers, including the temptation to convert qualitative to quantitative data, the difficulty of analysing temporal or socio-linguistic aspects of data, and the loss of the 'untypable'. These genuine dangers should be balanced against the genuine benefits of increased efficiency, flexibility and ease of retrieval.

Current CAQDAS software significantly limits the 'richness' of the data that can be analysed (Mason 1996). The primary way in which 'richness' is lost is through the decontextualisation of data by CAQDAS software. Code-and-retrieve methods of data analysis, both manual and computerised, break up data into chunks, and these chunks are sorted into groups according to the categories to which they relate. CAQDAS software makes this process much faster and easier. While most programs allow the researcher to view retrieved chunks within the context of surrounding sentences, the code-and-retrieve methodology encourages short segments of data to be viewed out of context, and not clearly linked to the more general interpretive frames utilised by the participant. The term 'rich data' derives from the term 'thick description' described initially by Geertz (1973). Thick description provides detail and background information that allows readers to understand the more general cultural patterns and meanings that make the described actions logical. Rich data include references that explain the relationship of the events under description to a more general cultural and interpretive framework. Miles and Huberman point out that a feature of 'qualitative data is their richness and holism, with a strong potential for revealing complexity; such data provide "thick descriptions" that are vivid, nested in a real context, and have a ring of truth that has a strong impact on the reader' (Miles & Huberman 1994: 10).

In a confusing analysis of this issue Richards (1999) equates rich data not with 'thick description' but with 'rich text', complex coding processes, and the ability to update documents during analysis. Rich text is text that includes formatting, such as colour, underlining, bold and italics. In one sense, rich text can be used to enrich data by using formatting to indicate emotion and other aspects difficult to represent in plain text documents. However, rich text is clearly an entirely different thing from the thick description described by Geertz. Sophisticated coding procedures may actually work against thick description if they encourage large numbers of codes. The danger here, as J. Daly suggests, is that 'the codes rather than the context become the focus of analysis' (1997: 3). Further, Mason (1996) and Barry (1998) both point out that it is not the complexity of coding but the coding process itself that decontextualises data, and makes it 'thin'. Coding segments and retrieving all the coded segments into one new composite document separates off the coded segments from the interpretive whole in which they originally occur. 'Thick description' requires that these coded segments be interpreted not only in comparison to other similarly coded segments but in the light of the interpretive framework in which they were originally presented. There are considerable benefits to the inclusion of rich text, complex coding procedures, and the ability to update documents mid-analysis, in new CAQDAS packages. These do not, however, solve the problem of the potential for CAQDAS packages to 'thin' the data due to the decontextualisation of small segments.

Some researchers have expressed fears that a CAQDAS package may distance them from the data and that the package may hijack the analysis. These fears may stem from lack of experience with CAQDAS packages (Barry 1998). When individuals who express these fears begin to use the technology, 'their negative perceptions were usually replaced by positive ones and an enthusiasm for positive ways in which the technology could help them'

(Barry 1998: 2.4). Similarly, research among users suggests that researchers tend to stop using a specific software package rather than allowing it to hijack their analysis (Lee & Fielding 1996).

The separation of data and the interpretive process is tacitly assumed in CAQDAS packages. Data typically cannot be altered once entered in the program, and memos, where theoretical reflections may be recorded, are typically created and edited as documents separate from the 'data' that are coded and analysed. Lindberg (1999) argues that computer-assisted analysis of qualitative data encourages what he provocatively terms 'naive inductivism'. He suggests that the use of software to assist in data analysis can lead to a preoccupation with what the data say, at the expense of examining how the emerging patterns might be related to existing theory. This is facilitated by programs that encourage the use of everyday language in developing categories and theory, which encourages a low level of abstraction. That is to say, CAQDAS packages do not appear to support the more theoretically informed and semiotic analyses of cultural studies and some feminist researchers. However, Lindberg provides no evidence to substantiate this claim and, indeed, emphasises that it is not the programs themselves, but the way they are used, that results in naive inductivism.

Some research reports appear to assume that if the computer package utilised for analysis is named, no further description of the method of analysis is required. Statements like 'the data [were] analysed with the Ethnograph software' (Long & Curry 1998: 205) and 'data were analysed using NUD*IST qualitative analysis program' (Eyler et al. 1998: 640) imply that there is a link between the choice of program and the type of analysis conducted. If a paper describing a quantitative study reported 'analysis was performed using Statistical Package for Social Sciences (SPSS)', readers of the paper would want to know which, of the large number of statistical techniques available in SPSS, had been performed. In the papers cited, one utilised content analysis, and the other thematic analysis. However, a statement to this effect is found only in the methodology section, whereas the name of the computer program appears in the abstract of the article. This suggests a misunderstanding of the role of the CAQDAS package, which does not perform the analysis but merely assists it.

Advocates of CAQDAS are quick to sell the good points of

the packages, and rarely admit to the dangers, difficulties and shortcomings. Kelle observes that economic competition between software developers may lead to an exaggerated estimation of the abilities of software programs: the developers are motivated 'to present straightforward techniques of data management as ground breaking methodological innovations' (Kelle 1997: 6.3). For example, the newsletter of one CAQDAS software package claims: 'Qualitative software has remade qualitative coding. Manual methods were often onerous, unreliable, and most importantly, an analytical dead-end. In the new software coding is swift, rigorous and leads on to asking further questions, refining ideas and developing theory' (Qualitative Solutions Research 1999: 1). The efficiencies and benefits of CAQDAS packages for certain types of analysis are rightly celebrated. However, despite the many innovations, Kelle is surely correct when he observes that 'these new programs (which often represent new and expanded versions of simple code-and-retrieve programs) do not provide a totally different logic of textual data management, but only more or less complicated extensions of code-and-retrieve facilities' (1997: 2.7).

Summary reflections

The value of computer-assisted analysis should not be underestimated. It greatly increases the efficiency and ease of code-and-retrieve procedures. However, computer-assisted analysis may not be useful for particular types of analysis and for particular types of data. One of the reasons that analytic procedures have not been formalised in some qualitative methods is that analysis is an interpretive process that is more akin to an artistic endeavour than a routine method, particularly when influenced by the more hermeneutic and interpretive research traditions. CAQDAS packages streamline the systematic and routine aspects of analysis, and this may provide a better foundation for the interpretive process, but they do not, and cannot, replace the interpretive, integrative, artistic and aesthetic components of the analytic process. The two sides of CAQDAS packages can be best understood with an example from the research literature.

Carmel (1999) describes the use of a CAQDAS package to analyse documents in a study of social policy in Germany. A combination of internal (electronic) and external (paper)

135

documents were coded and the coding entered in the package. Carmel identifies a number of advantages and problems associated with using the software. The search tools of the program were particularly useful in collating various combinations of codes and enabling the identification of changes peculiar to particular time periods. The ability to 'contextualise' data was 'particularly useful': 'The mass of data was transformed into a tractable object of interrogation, as the software provided easy access to overarching patterns (and vital exceptions to them)' (Carmel 1999: 147). Carmel was able to use the program to 'play' and 'experiment' with ideas and codes. The flexibility of the software allowed easy merging and recoding, and enhanced the process of exploration and experimentation. The memo facility was also useful, both as a mechanism for reflecting on the data and as a way of keeping track of the coding process.

However, the difficulties associated with coding paper documents led Carmel to 'a tactical decision to reduce the load of coding work by limiting the types of document to be coded' (1999: 146). This loss of data is a significant negative consequence of the choice to use a CAQDAS program. The reason for eliminating paper documents from the analysis derived from the flexibility in coding encouraged by the program. When codes are separated or merged, the program automatically updates all codes on the documents in the analysis. However, the external paper documents were coded manually, and every recode involved a laborious physical re-examination. The use of the CAQDAS package improved some aspects of the analysis, but restricted other aspects.

As with most new technology, there are always losses associated with new developments. Simplistic appraisals of CAQDAS software as either unambiguously beneficial or unequivocally useless are clearly misplaced. I use CAQDAS software as one of my research tools. I am aware of its limitations, ambivalent about its benefits and pleased by its effectiveness!

Further reading

Demonstration versions

CAQDAS networking project <http://caqdas.soc.surrey.ac.uk>

General discussions of the use of CAQDAS software

Fielding, N. and Lee, R. 1998 *Computer Analysis and Qualitative Research*, London, Sage.

Kelle, U. 1997 'Theory building in qualitative research and computer programs for the management of textual data' *Sociological Research Online*, vol. 2, no. 2, <http://www.socresonline.org.uk/socresonline/2/2/1.html>

Miles, M. and Huberman, A. 1994 *Qualitative Data Analysis: A Sourcebook of New Methods*, 2nd edn, Thousand Oaks, Sage.

Detailed reviews of the value of CAQDAS software for particular projects

Barry, C. 1998 'Choosing qualitative data analysis software: Atlas/ti and Nudist compared' *Sociological Research Online*, vol. 3, no. 3, <http://www.socresonline.org.uk/socresonline/3/3/4.html>

Carmel, E. 1999 'Concepts, context and discourse in a comparative case study' *International Journal of Social Research Methodology*, vol. 2, no. 2, pp. 141–50.

MacMillan, K. and McLachlan, S. 1999 'Theory-building with Nud.Ist: using computer assisted qualitative analysis in a media case study' *Sociological Research Online*, vol. 4, no. 2, <http://www.socresonline.org.uk/socresonline/4/2/macmillan_mcLachlan.html>

6

Writing about qualitative data

Shakespeare . . . was the man who of all modern, and perhaps ancient poets, had the largest and most comprehensive soul . . . when he describes anything, you more than see it, you feel it too (Dryden 1668, quoted in Sansom 1959: 82).

It is in writing that I have been able to link autobiography, biography and theory; in writing that I have decided what will and will not be significant; in writing that I have connected ideas to make arguments (Garrett 1998: 29).

Writing is at the heart of the research process. For many people discovery occurs in writing as much as it does during the tasks of data analysis. Writing is not simply about transferring 'results' to a written page. Writing is as much about creating 'results' as it is about reporting them. In the hermeneutic circle described in Chapter 1, I pointed out that data collection and analysis informs the development of new theory and interpretation. Writing is part of the interpretive process through which the theoretical implications of data collection and data analysis are worked out more fully, though never completely.

My image of the set of information that I obtain during a research project is of a multidimensional tangled ball of wool. There are many threads that interweave through the complex set of interviews, reflections and observations. The task of writing is to reconstruct this multifaceted, multidimensional ball of information into a linear story with a beginning, middle and end. The written report cuts a single line, or thread, through the complex ball of understanding. The best writing achieves this task of providing a well-written story while retaining a sense of the complexity and nuance suggested by the image of the ball of understanding. One way of doing this is to regularly refer to earlier parts of the research report. This reminds the reader that what they are currently reading is not only related to what came before and what comes after but is also linked in a multidimensional way to various other parts of the story.

As the above image suggests, writing research reports necessarily involves omitting many details, insights and complexities. Decisions to omit topics, themes or issues must be made with respect to the central theme or focus of *the current report*. Imposing a linear order on a complex multidimensional reality results in a report that is necessarily imperfect, provisional, partial, historical and situated. This is inevitable. The task, however, is to select the information relevant to the particular issues and tasks that the report attempts to address.

There are many types of qualitative and ethnographic writing. Van Maanen (1988) identifies three main types of ethnographic writing: realist tales, confessional tales, and impressionist tales. Realist tales have been historically the dominant form of ethnography. They present an account of a culture that presumes authority and accuracy and completely ignores the role of the author in the production of the account. This is exemplified by the absence of the word 'I' from these accounts. Confessional tales 'focus far more on the fieldworker than on the culture studied' (Van Maanen 1988: 7). They attempt to humanise the researcher through exposing his or her foibles and experiences. Impressionist writing draws on the two previous genres, in which dramatic experiential tales provide an account of the culture studied. Each of these styles selects a certain 'line' through the available information, addressing some issues and ignoring others.

Miller, Creswell and Olander's (1998) study of soup kitchens provides an excellent example of the movement from an objective realist analysis of research to a more critical and reflective awareness of the influence of the authors' experiences and the broader political and economic situatedness of their work. They show how the different theoretical assumptions brought to the data analysis task lead to different types of research reports. Modernist realist theory, such as that presented in many older qualitative methods textbooks, leads to a realist analysis of soup kitchens: 'Realist tales are characterized by the absence of the author, representation of the native's point of a view, and a documentary style' (Miller et al. 1998: 471). However, when a theoretical framework was utilised that highlighted the role of the researcher in the research, this led to a 'confessional tale' in which the researchers reveal their biases, mistakes and the experience of discovery. Finally, when confronted with an audience that asked questions about the relationship of the research to more general social issues of inequality, social justice and economics, they reported a very different analysis of their research that addressed these aspects.

This chapter moves from advice about the practicalities of writing up data to a more general discussion of the political and ethical implications of doing and writing qualitative research. The first half of the chapter reviews the process of writing, the importance of identifying an audience, varieties of writing styles, and the use of exemplars. The second half of the chapter begins with a discussion of whether reports should be written 'objectively', in the third person, and the implications of the 'representational crisis' for writing qualitative research. Experimental writing techniques are discussed along with whether to include personal experience in reports. A discussion of the ethics of writing about others leads into the issue of whether it is acceptable to categorise people in research reports. The final section brings the chapter full circle, back to some practical advice for writing reports for audiences other than academic audiences.

The process of writing: time, reflection and rhythm

> Speed, however, is not conducive to thinking . . . Thought calls for peace and rest, for 'taking one's time', recapitulating the steps already taken, looking closely at the place reached and the wisdom (or imprudence, as the case may be) of reaching it (Bauman 2000: 85).

Time is 'essential for the gestation of ideas' (Garrett 1998: 29). The reproductive metaphor of 'gestation' is appropriate. Ideas, new theory, new interpretations, are not discovered solely through the following of correct method, although this is an important part of the process. Rather, they are nurtured and discovered through a difficult process not unlike pregnancy and labour. Writing is the moment when ideas are finally given concrete form. Ideas must be nurtured and developed throughout the research process in journal entries, memos, new directions in questioning during interviews, literature searches and reflective moments. Time allows ideas to be explored, to be combined, pulled apart and recombined in thought. Without this time for gestation and development, the writing process will be difficult and the text stillborn!

It is important to create times for reflection, and to incorporate these into the routine of daily life. Some of my best insight comes while doing laps in the pool at the end of the day. Similarly, Garrett reports that most of her thinking about data analysis 'took place in the interstices of daily life; in the shower, driving to work, listening to music, gardening, reading apparently unrelated texts and talking to other people' (1998: 29).

I have found that one of the best ways to work out the central argument of an article or chapter that I am writing is to talk about it to friends and colleagues. In the act of talking my ideas become clearer, the structure of my argument becomes more developed and logical, and the potential problems begin to appear. Howard Becker explains that he typically begins to 'write' about something by talking about it in lectures, conference presentations and conversations with colleagues. Rather than writing rough drafts, Becker talks first drafts: 'I learned what points I could get to follow one another logically, which ways of making a point people understood, and which ways caused confusion, what arguments were dead ends that were better not entered at all' (1986: 101).

Well-planned writing should leave plenty of time for revision. Plenty of time for revision allows writing projects to be improved, with particular attention to the key areas of introductions and conclusions. As an undergraduate I noticed that the more time I left for writing, the longer I had to revise, and the better the mark I obtained. However, as an academic I have also noticed that when I repeatedly revise a paper I often reach a point where I am 'too close' to the paper to notice the mistakes. At this point, if I have time, I will put the paper aside for a week or so and then come back to it with 'fresh eyes'. Alternatively, I may ask a colleague to read the paper for me who will often notice problems and areas requiring work that I had missed.

Not everyone writes in the same way. Lofland and Lofland differentiate 'steady plodders and grand sweepers' (1971: 140).

Steady plodders write a little each day, slowly building up their analysis through writing about the details. Grand sweepers work first on the general outline of their writing, organising and detailing subsections and subcategories until a time comes when they work long and hard to turn the outline into a detailed written report.

Whichever writing style you adopt, Lofland and Lofland also advise that 'creating a serious outline' is well worth the effort (1971: 140). I find that sometimes I am able to see the overall outline of an article or report before I begin writing; at other times it is only well after I have begun to write that the overall structure becomes clear.

My own writing style is somewhere between steady plodder and grand sweeper. With large writing projects such as books or a series of articles, I try to work in cycles. I work hard for five days a week, and typically do not work on the weekends. I work hard for two or three weeks, perhaps working also at night, and then work one or two weeks of shorter days. Modern life treats people like machines. It assumes that we can work the same speed all day every day. I cannot work like this. It requires self-discipline to work hard, and this is something that can be learnt and cultivated. I find that I work most effectively and efficiently if I cycle through periods of working hard and periods of rest.

Writing a research report at the end of the project is much easier if you have been writing since the beginning of the research (see the section on journals and memos in Chapter 3). Mills advised some time ago: 'Many creative writers keep journals; the sociologist's need for systematic reflection demands it' (1959: 216). Like memos, an analytic journal contains records of thoughts, links to theory, ideas for analysis and early sections of preliminary analysis. Analysis is best done while the researcher is immersed in the data. For example, during the coding of the data I sometimes review a particular coding category, reading through all the relevant coded sections at that time. As I do this I build a summary understanding of that code in my mind. It is very helpful if I go the extra mile and write this summary down, along with a few selected excerpts from the transcripts. This means that when I am writing up the research I do not have to 'double-handle' the data. I already have the summary of that code written, and draw on that during the writing up. Similarly, if I am reading a theoretical article and I begin to think about the links between the article and my own analysis, I find it very beneficial to write these ideas down. I will even try to write a few paragraphs as if they were part of the research report. Writing these sorts of ideas down as they occur has a number of benefits. It keeps up the habit of writing, of thinking analytically. It also provides a rich set of prewritten sections that can form the basis of a written report.

Identify your audience

One of the key questions that confronts researchers as they write is: who is my audience? During my postgraduate research I wrote a paper on Simone Weil's understanding of the meaning of work (Ezzy 1997). Peter Beilharz, then a reader in sociology at La Trobe University where I was studying, kindly read it for me. I cannot remember much of what he said when we met to discuss the paper, but I do remember one question he asked me: 'Who is your audience?'. I was trying to identify a journal that might be interested in publishing my essay. Beilharz's question suggested that I needed to approach the task the other way around. First I needed to identify which academic journal included articles that related to the topic, and then rewrite my own article to tackle the issues that would interest the readers of that journal. The trick, of course, is to find a journal that is interested in the very issues you want to examine.

'Ethnographies are written with particular audiences in mind and reflect the presumptions carried by authors regarding the attitudes, expectations, and backgrounds of their intended readers' (Van Maanen 1988: 25). Social researchers who fail to identify correctly the relevant audience for their report may find that they are not understood, or easily misunderstood. A paper written for a theory journal may be unintelligible to an audience of policy makers. The need to identify one's audience is one of the implications of the insight that: 'Understanding comes not from the subject who thinks, but from the other that addresses me' (Risser 1997: 208). Part of the task of writing is to participate in an ongoing conversation. If you write a journal article you are participating in a more general scholarly debate, and in a specific ongoing conversation among the editors and readers of the journal in which you publish your article. A different set of issues will be relevant for an article written for an audience of research participants, to be published in a newsletter for example.

I have now developed a strategy for writing articles for particular journal audiences. When I am writing a journal article, I first identify one or two journals that have published articles on similar issues. I then search the abstracts from the journal for topics related to my article. Reading these articles carefully allows me to identify past contributions to the conversation in which I wish to participate by publishing my article. The quality of an article does not derive only from whether it follows logically or is methodologically rigorous, but also from how well the article engages with scholarly conversations that have already begun on the topic discussed in the article. Reports for audiences such as participants or policy makers require a similar sort of sensitivity to the content of ongoing conversations to which the report attempts to make a contribution.

Writing styles

A thorough familiarity with the phrases and words that describe the topics and issues under study is an important part of any research. I find it useful to carefully define key terms, comparing these against related terms, drawing on dictionaries and relevant reference texts. Identifying the right phrase or term to describe a code or concept is a task over which some researchers spend considerable amounts of time. Finding the right word to describe a phenomenon is important so that the correct overtones and nuances are communicated.

'I know you will agree that you should present your work in as clear and simple language as your subject and your thought about it permit' (Mills 1959: 239). Contemporary social research still has some genres that revel in 'turgid and polysyllabic prose'. Mills suggests that the use of difficult language is not a product of the profundity and subtlety of the issues being discussed, but a product of social researchers' attempts to distance themselves from journalism, to appear 'scientific', and hence to enhance their status. There is still a tendency for researchers to try to impress through the use of technical language and jargon, particularly under the influence of postmodernist and poststructuralist thought. While jargonised language is sometimes employed as a deliberate strategy to destabilise taken-for-granted understandings, it courts the danger of rendering the written text irrelevant to those who might find it useful. For example, a book reporting qualitative research on youth subjectivity may impress other scholars with its sophisticated understanding of French social theory. However, the insight it contains will be almost impossible to access for anyone without a PhD in the relevant area, such as youth workers or advisers to policy makers. Schwalbe (1995) observes that it makes sense that we should write for our colleagues, as they are the ones who primarily evaluate our work: However, writing only for our colleagues excludes other audiences that might benefit considerably from our work. 'Our first responsibility, then . . . is to make ourselves understood by the greatest number of people' (Schwalbe 1995: 397).

A good illustration of the sort of writing that combines theoretical complexity with accessibility is Lynne Hume's (1997) book on Paganism and Wicca in Australia based on extensive ethnographic fieldwork. She demonstrates a sophisticated anthropological theory and a sensitive understanding of Paganism in Australia. However, this sophistication is not demonstrated by complex jargon. Rather, the book is deceptively descriptive in its early parts, with engaging stories, interesting first-hand experiences, and intriguing accounts of the beliefs of pagans and witches. This apparent simplicity belies a sophisticated anthropological hermeneutic theory that becomes more apparent towards the end of the book, as she explores some of the more complex and nuanced issues associated with the nature of spiritual belief and practice. The sophistication of her theory is demonstrated through the subtlety of her handling of the subject matter rather than through an attempt to 'snow' the reader with complex and esoteric jargon. There are many other similar examples of well-written qualitative research, including Garrett's (1998) study of anorexia, Karp's (1996) study of depression, Irvine's (1999) study of codependency, and Snow and Anderson's (1993) study of homelessness.

These comments should not be read as an argument for the 'dumbing down' of sociological research reports. Rather, they are a call for a more sophisticated understanding of the audiences of social research reports, so that these reports can more easily be integrated in the ongoing dialogue of both academic and more general debates. There is a place for more jargonised, subtle and sophisticated language, such as Ricoeur's (1988) studies of narrative. However, as Mills observes, 'the line between profundity and verbiage is often delicate, and even perilous' (1959: 243).

The quote from Dryden at the opening of this chapter suggests that good writing does not merely describe something—good writing makes you feel it too. Schwalbe's description of Kai Erikson's (1976) ethnography of the Buffalo Creek disaster,

Everything in its Path, makes precisely this point. Erikson's book is an excellent example of the craft of well-written ethnography: 'It engages us, and evokes an emotional response, because it's full of vivid details and intelligent observations about real people, places, and events' (Schwalbe 1995: 403).

The detail of qualitative research reports is important. This is because, unlike quantitative reports, qualitative studies are concerned with nuance, shared understanding and the elaboration of meaning. Key statistical results can be summarised in an abstract, but the interpretive understanding that qualitative reports convey cannot be so easily summarised: 'Qualitative research has to be read, not scanned; its meaning is in the reading' (Richardson 1997: 87).

I tell my students that the most important part of an undergraduate essay is the first paragraph. It should be clear, grammatically correct and outline the structure of the argument of the essay. If the first paragraph impresses, this sets up an expectation in a reader's mind that the rest of the essay will be of a similar quality. If the first paragraph is confused, contains grammatical errors, and does not provide a clear outline of the essay, this sets up a corresponding expectation in the reader's mind. A well-written first paragraph is the equivalent of two or three well-written paragraphs in the body of the essay. Not only does the first paragraph establish expectations about the quality of the essay, it also establishes expectations about the content. If, from the introduction, it is clear that issues X, Y but not Z will be discussed in the essay, then when the reader finds issues X and Y discussed in subsequent paragraphs, they will not be concerned about the absence of Z, because they already know from the introduction that the essay is only about X and Y. It is not necessary for an introduction to state that 'Z will not be discussed in this essay'. There is no need to say what you are *not* going to write about. Rather, the introduction needs to state clearly that 'X and Y are the focus of this essay'. However, if the introduction makes some vague allusion to 'letters at the end of the alphabet', the reader will wonder why subsequent paragraphs about X and Y do not discuss Z.

This point works equally well for the first chapters of books and theses, the first paragraphs of subsequent chapters of books, the first sections of articles or reports and the first sentences of paragraphs. Clear introductions are a quintessential part of clear writing. At the other end, clear conclusions and summaries are equally important: they remind the reader of the important points that have been covered.

The use of exemplars

Most qualitative research reports include a mixture of theoretical analysis and illustrative extracts from the primary data. The report moves between the author's voice and a variety of other voices that are used as 'exemplars' to support the author's argument. Extracts usually serve as illustrations of more general theoretical propositions. Atkinson (1990) identifies three functions of these exemplars within ethnographic texts. First, through detailed description exemplars allow the reader to enter an imagined experience of the described culture and social world. Second, exemplars allow the introduction of a variety of voices and perspectives to the text. Finally, exemplars allow participants, along with the author and the reader, to participate in the collaborative construction of the text's meaning.

Displaying segments of primary texts in research reports makes the primary data on which the analysis is built available to other researchers. Other researchers are then able to assess the trustworthiness of the interpretations of these data made by the analyst. Mishler (1990) argues that the presentation of primary textual data in qualitative reports serves a similar function to 'exemplars' or concrete solutions to research problems in practice that guide natural science research programs (Mishler 1990). Mishler goes on to argue that qualitative studies, and for that matter statistical studies as well, do not rely solely on following the rules and procedures of a method to guarantee that research will be valued by other researchers. Rather, reliability and validity in statistical studies, and rigour in qualitative studies, are rhetorical strategies designed to convince an audience of scholars that the results of the study are worthy of being trusted.

For example, in my comparison of ecological and economic narratives (Ezzy 2000c) I conducted a thematic analysis of four mainstream journals. I quote from these journals to illustrate the more general argument I make about the way economic narratives differ from ecological narratives:

> Ecological narratives contain images of impending destruction that emphasise the limited nature of human choice. For example, Bunyard (1999) points out that feedback loops in the global climate could lead to climate change spiralling out of control, and that we have very limited choices if we are to prevent 'deadly destruction' . . . [in contrast] the economist's vision of the future is of progress, and increasing wealth. Always ameliorated by the heroic need to bear

pain in the short term, the long view is unambiguously optimistic. Hammonds (1998: 85) suggests that there will be some 'brutal lows' along the way, but 'ultimately we're likely to be just fine' (Ezzy 2000c: 185).

Note how the text moves back and forth between general statements about the structure of the narratives and specific examples of these narratives. The exemplars introduce the voices of both economists and ecologists alongside my own. The quotes serve the rhetorical purpose of convincing the reader that the general argument about the nature of ecological and economic narratives is indeed easily identifiable in individual examples.

Although the two quotes above are short, I do provide some longer illustrative quotes that allow the reader to enter into the argument of the ecologists and economists. Atkinson (1990) argues that illustrations such as these should not be seen as statistically representative cases, but as rhetorical devices that clearly exhibit the tendencies described in the surrounding texts. Extreme cases or particularly revealing illustrations may be selected and presented in the text. The point is not to provide a typical case, but to convince through enabling the reader to identify and participate in the process of constructing a similar interpretation of the ethnographic evidence. Typical cases would be expected to reveal similar tendencies, but perhaps less obviously or less strikingly.

Objectivity and the representational crisis

The traditional modernist understanding of qualitative research includes a strong distinction between fact and fiction, and between facts and values. This approach argues that research reports should present objective facts, established by scientific methodology, and that values should be left out of the report. However, as Mishler (1990) points out, literary devices such as metaphor, image and narrative are integral to the reporting of scientific findings. In a similar way, Ricoeur (1988) demonstrates that history is quasi-fictive, drawing on literature to provide models for compositional form and to represent history to the imagination.

A written research report is both less than, and more than, the events it represents. It is less than the events it represents because it can never provide an account of the complexity and nuances that arise during interaction. Observing, and writing, are acts of selective attention. They represent experiences and action from the standpoint of the observer. Reports highlight some aspects of a phenomenon and suppress others.

Research reports are also more than the events they describe. This is because, as Ricoeur (1988) points out, events become meaningful only insofar as they are interpreted within the frame of a narrative, a story that accounts for the reasons and consequences of the described episodes. Writing is an act of constructing meaning. Without the interpretive plot provided by literary devices, the findings of research reports would become dull and irrelevant. Corbin and Strauss (1990) make this explicit in their discussion of selective coding that describes the task of identifying the central 'story' that emerges from the data. Clearly stories do not simply emerge, but are also selected from available repertoires derived from literature and the media.

Such an understanding of the intimate links between science and literature, between faction and fiction, does not lead to relativist scepticism but to a more sophisticated approach to social research. As Richardson suggests, rather than abandoning the claim to be doing science, 'we can lay claim to a science that is aesthetic, moral, ethical, moving, rich, and metaphoric as well as avant-garde, transgressing, and multivocal' (Richardson 1997: 16).

Traditional ethnography and qualitative research is realist. It assumes that what is said in a research report accurately mirrors the events in an external objective world:

> Critical poststructuralism challenges these assumptions. Language and speech do not mirror experience: they create experience and in the process of creation constantly transform and defer that which is being described (Denzin 1997: 5).

How can a qualitative research report presume to 'represent' the experience of, for example, people living with HIV/AIDS, if the very act of writing does not mirror but creates the experience of people living with HIV/AIDS? This crisis of representation can slip into a textual solipsism, where reality is irrelevant and all interpretations are equally valid, as was suggested in Chapter 1. In contrast, I argue that, rather than leading to relativism, the 'linguistic turn' requires social researchers to attend to the ongoing cyclical nature of reality and interpretation. As Lather (1993) has argued, the linguistic turn, or the crisis of representation, does not mean that representation is no longer possible; it simply means that it is no longer possible to pretend that any one particular representation is the one true, authoritative and accurate account for all time.

Traditional forms of ethnography pretended to be 'objective' and to transcend time and history as a consequence of being written in the third person, as if the author had no influence on the text that was presented. Traditional forms of qualitative reports also typically used the form of a realist tale to present the analysis as 'objective', as if the moral and political commitments of the researcher also had no influence on the production of the text.

Contemporary debates about the nature of academic writing in general, and qualitative writing in particular, suggest that traditional writing styles are problematic. For example, ethnography written exclusively in the third person of 'he', 'she' and 'they' does not do justice to the role of the researcher's self, the 'I', as an integral part of the research process. Poststructuralist and feminist thought in particular have highlighted the value of reflexivity, and of exploring ways of researching and writing that break with the mould of the traditional distanced, disengaged and stylistically stilted writing.

Poststructuralism has two important implications for qualitative writers according to Richardson: 'First, it directs us to understand ourselves reflexively as persons writing from particular positions at specific times; and second, it frees us from trying to write a single text in which everything is said to everyone' (1997: 89). The first point reminds us that, however much previous authors have tried to suppress it, the self is always an abiding influence in and on our writing. Bauman provocatively argues that the ideal of a 'neutral' sociology is a fallacy, and that all research is profoundly influenced by the identity, values and worldview of the researcher: 'A non-committal sociology is an impossibility' (2000: 89). The second point highlights the partial, situational, historical and provisional nature of all knowledge. There is no 'final' or 'correct' analysis. The patterns of human action are stable enough, and the frames of interpretation shared widely enough, to make the insights derived from qualitative social research valuable and insightful for participants, theorists and policy makers. This should never be allowed, however, to support the modernist conceit that the one final, ahistorical and complete analysis can be written.

Experimental writing

Experimental writing develops out of the influence of feminist and postmodernist criticisms of earlier ethnographic and qualitative research reporting. These experimental forms of writing are deliberate attempts to reposition the author and the reader. The new writing includes short stories (Ellis 1995a; Devault 1999), poetry (Brady 2000; Dickson 2000), personal narratives (Church 1995; Davidman 1999; Smith 2000) polyvocal texts (Lather 1997), along with a variety of other genres including drama, performance science, aphorisms, visual presentations, mixed genres and cybertexts (Richardson 1997). The 'freedom' these experimental forms appear to provide is deceptive. They do not automatically lead to better reports, or to greater insight. With the added burden of political and ethical issues raised by heightened reflexivity, and other dimensions such as questions of authorship and authenticity, experimental writing is harder work than more traditional forms (Glassner & Hertz 1999). Experimental writing problematises more dimensions, introduces greater uncertainty, and requires concurrent attentiveness to a wider range of issues. The rewards are rich, but the risks are also significant.

There has been considerable debate over the value of experimental forms of writing. Schwalbe (1995), for example, argues that it is a mistake to think that experimenting with different *forms* of writing will provide more evocative research reports. Rather, he argues that qualitative researchers need to write more engaging prose. The numbingly boring nature of some qualitative reports is not, he argues, a product of the form of the writing but the style of the writing. The solution, according to Schwalbe, is to write more engaging and evocative prose. More specifically, Schwalbe points out that where prose makes meanings explicit, poetry is more cryptic, relying on hidden meanings, and is more difficult to interpret. While poetry has some value, according to Schwalbe it cannot replace carefully crafted prose. Alternative modes of presentation run the risk of 'descent into "cleverness" and pretension' (Atkinson 1990: 180). Bauman (2000) argues that sociologists do not write poetry. However, he points out that poetry is similar to sociology because both aim to break down commonsense and obvious understanding. Like poetry, sociology aims to disclose new possibilities, opening up humanity to what might be.

In response to Schwalbe's criticism of sociological poets, Richardson (1996) and Denzin (1996b) argue that qualitative sociologists who experiment with different forms of writing should be encouraged. They suggest that Schwalbe's criticisms of sociological poetry are in danger of being exclusionary and of discouraging the creativity and experimentation that is at heart of the process of discovery. More specifically, Denzin points out that poetic texts attempt to engage with the changed understanding of reality and representation that has developed out of postmodernist theory.

While there is much to be learnt from an awareness of the literary and textual analysis of ethnographic writing, there is 'no need for sociologists all to flock towards "alternative" literary modes' (Atkinson 1990: 180). The argument here is not that all social researchers should become poets, novelists or dramatists. The skills required to succeed in these fields are not skills that social researchers seek to nurture: 'Rather, my intention is to encourage individuals to accept and nurture their own voices. The researcher's self-knowledge and knowledge of the topic develops through experimentation with point of view, tone, texture, sequencing, metaphor, and so on' (Richardson 1997: 93). The point is not that new modes of writing should be adopted wholesale; rather, that it is no longer possible to pretend that the way in which qualitative reports are written can be treated as straightforward: 'The fully mature ethnography requires a reflexive awareness of its own writing, the possibilities and limits of its own language, and a principled exploration of its modes of representation' (Atkinson 1990: 180).

In Chapter 4, I describe how coding involves a process of breaking apart data followed by a recombination that is continuous and cyclical. Discovery of new meanings and patterns in data involves exploration and experimentation with different combinations of codes. In a similar way, Richardson suggests that writing qualitative research involves experimenting with different literary devices such as 'point of view, tone, texture, sequencing, metaphor, and so on'. Like coding, writing involves looking at events and interpretations in a variety of ways until a story emerges from the creative engagement of researcher and participant.

However, the move to more 'experimental' forms and styles of writing is not without its problems. As Richardson (1997) observes, many older academics entrenched in senior positions resist these innovations. This can create a difficult tension for the early-career academic, who wants to explore innovative methods of research and writing, but also wants to succeed in academic institutions that may not value such efforts very highly. This does not mean that it is impossible to utilise innovative research methods and writing styles—rather that the consequences of adopting such innovative styles should be carefully weighed.

Including the personal experience of the researcher

> Leaving oneself open to the life-world of one's subjects means making oneself vulnerable (Liberman 1999: 50).

> You must learn to use your life experience in your intellectual work: continually to examine and interpret it (Mills 1959: 216).

Feminist researchers typically argue that the personal experience of the researcher is an integral part of the research process. Personal experience typically shapes the definition of the research problem and the method used to collect and analyse data. Personal experience is also a source of data about the research problem. More metaphorically, Cotterill and Letherby suggest that 'feminist research involves weaving the stories of both the researcher and her respondents' (1993: 67). Although the idea predates feminism, feminist methodology has significantly advanced the acceptability and plausibility of reflexively including the researcher's own experience as part of the research process. The inclusion of personal experience undermines, and problematises, the claim of research to be 'objective' or apolitical and the researcher to be detached and distanced. This, of course, links in with the aims of feminist and participatory research to explicitly include political objectives as part of the research. Including personal experience is still not accepted by all social researchers, particularly those who retain a commitment to a modernist or positivist conception of social research. This is illustrated most clearly in journal articles: 'Whereas feminist researchers frequently present their research in their own voice, researchers publishing in mainstream journals typically are forbidden to use the first person singular voice' (Reinharz 1992: 258). In contrast to positivist prohibitions of reports of personal experience, some feminist researchers have made the inclusion of personal experience mandatory, as a criterion for assessing the validity and legitimacy of feminist research (Mies 1991).

The feminist emphasis on placing the personal experience of the researcher within the research report has important implications for qualitative methods more generally. The incorporation of personal experience in qualitative methods extends from comments in a book's preface about how a researcher came to a topic, and his or her involvement in it, to the almost complete immersion of autoethnography (Ellis 1995b). In between are the more explicit attempts to locate the author's voice within a research report. Hertz (1996) argues that the issues of voice and reflexivity are central to contemporary qualitative research, and she demonstrates that dealing with these issues provides a similar function to traditional concerns about acting ethically towards respondents. The collection edited by Glassner and Hertz (1999) provides an excellent demonstration of the value and utility of explicitly reporting on qualitative research from the perspective and experience of the researcher's own everyday life.

Reflexively including the researcher in the research may involve all aspects of the research process. Personal experience provides data, ideas for theories, contacts for research subjects, it shapes the methodology, conduct of fieldwork and data analysis, and can be an important part of the research report. A clear example of this last aspect is provided by Lather and Smithies (1997), whose book often contains pages split horizontally, with analysis of their participants across the top of the page, and notes from the researchers' journals describing their personal responses across the bottom of the page. The role of the researcher is explicitly part of the research: 'We have written a book about others who both are and are not like ourselves, as we give testimony to what are our own stories and larger than our own lives' (Lather & Smithies 1997: xiv).

Writing the self into research reports enhances the authenticity of the research (Mishler 1986). Feminists such as Stanley have suggested that this form of reflexivity should involve 'focusing on the processes by which evaluations, interpretations and conclusions have been reached from whatever "data" I have worked on, including my auto/biographical work' (Stanley 1993: 43). Writing oneself into one's research is not a form of self-indulgence. Rather, it is a disciplined approach to addressing the role of researchers in their research. This does not mean that all forms of autobiography in research reports are acceptable or useful. What constitutes appropriate autobiography is still a matter of some debate (Mykhalovskiy 1996). However, it is now an issue that requires engagement, and cannot plausibly be avoided through retreat into a discourse of detached objectivity.

Qualitative research is an explicit attempt to engage self and other in conversation. From a hermeneutic perspective, Ricoeur (1992) argued that we become a self through our relationships with the other. In qualitative research we engage this self–other nexus to learn more about the other, to hear their voice. Research reports that do not disclose the role of the researcher no longer have a ring of authenticity to many researchers (Reinharz 1992): 'Self and Other are knottily entangled. This relationship, as lived between researchers and informants, is typically obscured in social science texts, protecting privilege, securing distance, and laminating the contradictions' (Fine, M. 1994: 72).

To explicitly address the issue of the role of the researcher in the research promises to provide 'better data' (Fine, M. 1994: 72). This is because it explicitly engages with the hermeneutic circle of the construction of knowledge. Understanding is accomplished as part of a conversation. To erase, or ignore, the role of one of the participants in this conversation (i.e. the researcher) provides a limited and tendentious account of both the research and the researched. The conscious inclusion of the researcher's own subjectivity is one practice that replaces the rhetoric of value-free objectivity. Feminists argue that the inclusion of personal experience is not only 'more honest' but 'helps to break down the power relationship between researcher and researched' (Cotterill & Letherby 1993: 71).

Including autobiographical details in research reports raises a number of problems. Unlike traditional researchers who write themselves out of their reports, and unlike research subjects who are protected by assurances of confidentiality and anonymity, a researcher's name is now clearly linked to the publication. This can be problematic when dealing with controversial or sensitive topics. Cotterill and Letherby report that, although one of them is committed to the inclusion of her own experiences in her research, she finds discussing her own experience of 'involuntary childlessness' and 'infertility' problematic. While she is 'happy to talk about these issues with "specific" people, she will not always be able to pick her audience and feels apprehensive and embarrassed about the "world at large" seeing her wear her "heart on her sleeve"' (Cotterill & Letherby 1993: 73). While personal experience is a rich source of information and enhances authenticity, reporting personal experiences is not always unproblematic. As with all disclosure of participants' experience in qualitative reports, disclosure of the researcher's experience should weigh the benefits of disclosure, such as increased plausibility and rich data, against the costs, such as public exposure of potentially confidential information. Again, rather than presuming that it is acceptable to ignore the researcher's role in the research, in the light of feminist commentary it is now incumbent on researchers to take seriously how they use and report their own role in their research.

The ethics of writing about others

> She had asked for a copy of the book I had written about her and the others. I gave it to her as a gift. She had just read what I had written about her ten years before. She was wounded by the images of herself in the past—psychotic, rambling, wise, and charming. I had exploited her, used her, misunderstood everything, and was unmasked now, she said. Not the bright 'liberal', sympathetic researcher I claimed to be, but worse than the others for my self- and other deception. Furthered my career, made a name for myself, all at her expense. How could you? (Estroff 1995: 77).

> I could not do a community study like *Street Corner Society*. I wouldn't want to take responsibility for how I brought the 'community' into my text (theory, debates, and so on); I wouldn't want to 'give voice' to real, live people who know each other and could identify each other in my text. For me, it might be 'text'; for them, it is life . . . [However] You see, an ethnographic project beckons me. There is this Park of Roses (Richardson 1997: 117).

In the quote above Richardson begins by saying that she could not conduct an ethnography like Whyte's *Street Corner Society*, and then she goes on to describe just such an ethnography that beckons her. The first step in writing responsibly about others is to acknowledge precisely this tension. Representing other people's lives is a risky and difficult business, but is also profoundly rewarding and worthwhile. When a participant signs a consent form, this is not the end of our responsibilities but the beginning. Many research participants are vulnerable and relatively powerless. To conduct research with, and to write about, such people is to enter into a relationship of responsibility with them.

All writing is integrally political and moral (Taylor 1989). The task, therefore, is not to attempt to avoid political or moral issues but to write with an awareness of political and moral implications. Estroff argues that it is possible to write so as to 'increase the opportunity for mutual benefit and reduce the chances for harms and wrongs' (1995: 97). Bauman makes this point succinctly:

> Doing sociology and writing sociology are aimed at disclosing the possibility of living together differently, with less misery or no misery: the possibility daily withheld, overlooked or unbelieved. Not-seeing, not-seeking and thereby suppressing this possibility is itself part of human misery and a major factor in its perpetuation (Bauman 2000: 89).

Writing qualitative research involves participating in an ongoing dialogue. This dialogue is necessarily political, ethical and moral. Some reports, and some issues within those reports, will be more politically sensitive than others. The task of the qualitative research is not to attempt to solve political and moral issues, nor to avoid them, but to be aware of and engage with the potential political and moral implications of their writings.

The political implications of categorising people

The political nature of research reports is well demonstrated in the debate about classifying people, and their experiences, into shared categories. Categorising people and their experiences is at the heart of qualitative data analysis, and the debate around these issues illustrates the concerns that should be kept in mind while writing reports.

The classification of people into particular categories is politically problematic because to categorise people implies that people similarly categorised will have similar experiences that can inform social policy (Somers & Gibson 1994). The clearest example of the problematic nature of categorising is where researchers assume that research results from studies with male participants will apply also to women, because they both fit in the category 'person'. Early feminists such as Chodorow (1978) attempted to develop a different analysis of women's experience that celebrates the feminine. However, the same error is made on another level: feminists of colour, for example, point out that feminist identity theory oversimplifies their experience. Results from research with white women may not be valid for black women. The experiences of women of different class, sexual identity and age are also marginalised in early feminist identity theory. For every categorisation there will always be a subgroup whose experience may not be represented by the categorisation.

Lemert, in a provocative paper called 'Dark thoughts about the self' (1994), takes this analysis a step further, identifying two main groups of thinkers about the self and shared experiences. Strong-we theorists (William James, G.H. Mead, Charles Taylor, Craig Calhoun and Ken Gergen—all male, white and heterosexual) present a strong position because they enforce 'the illusion that humanity itself constitutes the final and sufficient identifying group' (Lemert 1994: 104). Weak-we thinkers, including Patricia Collins, Jeffrey Weeks and the late modern interactionists (Katovich & Reese 1993), locate a 'practical meaningful sense of oneself in concrete historical relations with local groups' (Lemert 1994: 104). Local associations and histories are much more significant to these people than any universal or global humanity. That is to say, Lemert suggests that, on the one hand, strong-we theorists are willing to put people together into a global shared category called 'humanity', which forms the basis for shared human values. On the other hand, weak-we theorists refuse to accept that there is any global category and so reject the idea of global or transcendent values.

The strong-we theorists attempt to universalise particular characteristics of self-narratives. Their stories of a unified self reflect the cultural positioning of these theorists. The strong-we theorists attempt to generate a universal claim on all humans. Whether this is cognitive (Mead), existential, and hence moral (Taylor), or historicist, all identify a universal moral self. However, these theorists have a dark secret:

> No proponent of the strong-we position can admit the legitimate claims of those in the weak-we position, whatever he may see or believe. Such an admission destroys the moral claims whereby a local culture presents itself as though it were universal. Dark secrets, whether in culture or individual character, must be kept in silence' (Lemert 1994: 116).

Being human, Lemert argues, does not lead to a common form of shared self-understanding or experience. The two are ontologically separate, and the strong-we theorists produce a sleight of hand when they assume that all humans share particular characteristics. Lemert calls for analysis to begin on a more concrete historical plane in order to avoid the problems of the strong-we theorists.

However, Lemert's call for avoiding all claims to universal or shared experiences is not as straightforward as it may seem. Calhoun (1994) argues that categorisations of identities are always problematic because they are unavoidably political acts. According to Calhoun, essentialist claims about identities are often used and justified as political tactics. If it is impossible to conduct social analysis without categories, it therefore is impossible to avoid making some sort of essentialist claims about identities. Lemert is right to point out that strong-we theorists pretend that their analyses cover all human experience when they do not. However, this does not mean that we should never attempt to categorise people into groups of shared experience. The inherently political nature of social life means that the use of categories to describe group experience is unavoidable. The point is to be critically aware of the political implications of such categorisations: they should not be dark secrets, so much as acknowledged political claims.

The problem, according to Somers and Gibson (1994), lies in the assumption that people similarly categorised will have similar experiences and share common understandings of their experiences. They argue that the empirical identification of shared narrative interpretations solves this problem. Shared narrative interpretations are shared events that are a product of shared relational settings and understandings that will lead to common goals and actions. In short, interests and understandings cannot be imputed to people on the basis of shared categorisation. Rather, to the extent that categories are used, they need to be empirically and inductively derived from shared narratives.

Categorising people according to shared experiences or interpretations is an inherently political act. Categories are often used to describe the experiences of various subgroups who may not share all the characteristics assumed by the categorisation. Building categorisations up through inductive empirical research is one solution to the problem of categorisation. However, even this does not prevent the problems of unwarranted overgeneralisation of the applicability of categories. Rather than trying to avoid the political consequences of categorising, the more pragmatic approach is to acknowledge the political implications explicitly, incorporating them in the research.

Academic publications and community reporting

Many researchers produce community or policy reports. I view the writing of these reports as an important opportunity to provide some substantive return to my research subjects. Kathryn Church's (Church & Creal 1995; Church 1997) work is a good example of this genre, but there are many others. These are research reports that provide the research findings in an accessible language to the relevant community members and/or policy makers. While it means writing up the research in different ways, it is important to recognise the requirements of academic audiences who read peer-reviewed journals, as opposed to those of policy makers and community members, who are more concerned with information that will allow them to argue for additional funding, the redirection of services or the need for new strategies.

Community and policy reports provide and maintain the credibility of a researcher or research organisation among the community groups who may be involved in future research. For example, of the people living with HIV/AIDS that I interviewed, many complained that researchers would come in, do their survey or interview and never be heard from again. The results may have been reported in a thesis bound in a university library somewhere, or in a difficult-to-access academic journal in language hard to understand for these participants. The research team I was involved in at the National Centre in HIV Social Research at La Trobe University had a tradition of community consultation and writing community reports (e.g., see Ezzy et al. 1997; Ezzy et al. 1998). We found that community reports were valued by the community. The reports provided the research results in a more accessible format that could be utilised to inform ongoing projects and advocacy. One of the consequences of the regular production of community reports was that community organisations continued to provide ongoing input and support for new research projects.

Community or policy reports do not involve the level of direct political action advocated by some feminist action-oriented research. Nonetheless, the attempt to engage with relevant communities through the provision of information has similar sorts of problems to feminist action-oriented research. Coates and associates point out that feminist action-oriented research is often avoided by academics for three reasons: '(a) it jeopardizes one's academic status and chances of getting tenure; (b) it is too much work to meet university requirements and ethical and political ones as well; and (c) granting councils do not value activist research and will not support it financially' (Coates et al. 1998: 340). Some of these points are also relevant to the less critical but nonetheless politically engaged commitment to writing community or policy reports. While funding bodies may provide funds for community reports and to facilitate the participation of the community in the research, these have to be carefully justified in terms of the research goals, and even then are likely to be seen as an unnecessary addition. Further, while community and policy reports are different from refereed journal articles, they may count very little or not at all when it comes to academic indicators of progress. This means there are very few academic incentives for writing community or policy reports. While it is possible for policy or community documents to be politically sensitive, the effect on academic progress is more likely to be indirect—through the proportionally less time available for the all-important refereed journal articles that are often the primary indicator of academic success.

Summary reflections

Writing qualitative research is difficult, but rewarding. Issues raised by feminists and poststructuralists have further complicated the decisions researchers must make in choosing how to write a research report. To acknowledge that qualitative reports have political consequences is relatively easy. The more difficult task is to write reports that constructively participate in those political processes. To acknowledge that you, the researcher, have had a hand in not only writing but creating the data on which a report is based is relatively straightforward. More challenging is the task of untangling the personal, communal and theoretical implications of this interpretive approach.

Writing, like data analysis, can be improved by following the methods and using some of the practical techniques described in this chapter. Taking time to reflect, locating your audience, adjusting your writing style and making careful use of examples are all important. Good writing depends on an appreciation of the practices of others, of the techniques for writing well.

Beyond these methodological practices are other factors such as a passion for discovery, a sensitivity to the voice of the 'other', and a compassionate appreciation of the shared joy and pain of life. These things, however, cannot be taught in a textbook, and I have made no attempt to describe them here. I can not imagine how I might communicate them through a written text—although maybe through a novel or a poem. It is these ineffable aspects that sit behind, or imbue, the best qualitative writing. I cried when I read David Karp's (1996) *Speaking of Sadness*. Perhaps, in part, it was because the book brought to the surface some strongly felt emotions relating to a close friend with clinical depression. However, it was also because, for me, it communicated that difficult-to-pin-down quintessence that is a characteristic of the very best qualitative research.

Further reading

General guides to writing reports

Bauman, Z. 2000 'On writing sociology' *Theory, Culture and Society*, vol. 17, no. 1, pp. 79–90.
Becker, H. 1986 *Writing for Social Scientists*, Chicago, University of Chicago Press.
Mills, C. 1959 *The Sociological Imagination*, Harmondsworth, Penguin.
Richardson, L. 1994 'Writing: a method of inquiry' in N. Denzin and Y. Lincoln (eds) *Handbook of Qualitative Research*, Thousand Oaks, Sage, pp. 516–29.

Including the researcher in the research

Davidman, L. 1999 'The personal, the sociological, and the intersection of the two' in B. Glassner and R. Hertz (eds) *Qualitative Sociology as Everyday Life*, Thousand Oaks, Sage, pp. 79–87.
Devault, M. 1999 'Are we alone?' in B. Glassner and R. Hertz (eds) *Qualitative Sociology as Everyday Life*, Thousand Oaks, Sage, pp. 89–96.
Estroff, S. 1995 'Whose story is it anyway?' in S. Toombs, D. Barnard and R. Carson (eds) *Chronic Illness: From Experience to Policy*, Bloomington, Indiana University Press, pp. 77–102.

Examples of 'new' qualitative writing

Brady, I. 2000 'Three jaguar/Mayan intertexts: poetry and prose
    fiction' *Qualitative Inquiry*, vol. 6, no. 1, pp. 58–65.
Church, K. 1995 *Forbidden Narratives: Critical Autobiography as
    Social Science*, Luxembourg, Gordon & Breach.
Dickson, G. 2000 '"Aboriginal grandmothers" experience with
    health promotion and participatory action research'
    Qualitative Health Research, vol. 10, no. 2, pp. 188–213.
Ellis, C. 1995a 'Speaking of dying: an ethnographic short story'
    Symbolic Interaction, vol. 18, no. 1, pp. 73–81.
Lather, P. 1997 'Drawing the line at angels: working the ruins of
    feminist ethnography' *Qualitative Studies in Education*,
    vol. 10, no. 3, pp. 285–304.
Smith, B. 1999 'The abyss: exploring depression through a
    narrative of the self' *Qualitative Inquiry*, vol. 5, no. 2,
    pp. 264–82.

Concluding reflections

> Questioning is . . . a probing of possibilities . . . For Gadamer the point is not so much that questions then get answered . . . but that in questioning I am able to gain access to the otherness of the other (Risser 1997: 137).

What is my political agenda? What is the dialogue to which I hope this book will contribute? Poststructuralist and postmodernist theory, feminist methodology and hermeneutics are still largely ignored by mainstream social researchers. If qualitative research is considered a second-class citizen in the social research community, then these more recent approaches are at least third-class citizens. I argue that the way forward for qualitative research is to incorporate these new methods in the qualitative cannon. I am a syncretist. I have tried to offer compromises, composite methodologies, that listen to both sides of the argument and move forward through dialogue and incorporation.

On my wall at home I have a print of Hieronymous Bosch's painting *The Garden of Earthly Delights*. It is a wonderful yet weird picture, mixing images of ecstatic pleasures, such as cavorting nude bathers, oversized strawberries and angelic musicians, with images of hellish torture, such as men impaled on knives or being eaten and defecated by massive insects. The challenge of the painting is that its interpretation is impossible to resolve. One group of art historians argue it represents the values of the early sixteenth century during which it was painted, condemning

164

pleasure-seekers. Another group of interpreters argue that Bosch was a member of a heretical sect who secretly celebrated pleasure, and particularly sexual pleasure (Fontana 1997). Bosch wrote nothing, and we know almost nothing about his life other than the bare details. This is a text without an authoritative authorial interpretation. It encourages us, even forces us, to acknowledge that the way we interpret the picture is not based on historical evidence, but on our own interpretive predilections. As I look at the painting, and the interpretive conundrum whirls within me, the uncertainty, the enforced subjectivity, actually becomes a pleasure in itself:

> Ultimately Bosch remains an unknown, defying categorizing and objective analyzing, and this is the beauty of the text; it unravels forever as a new story to be told again and again and again. Bosch and the painting are, in their radical uncertainty, an archetypal example of the pains and pleasures of textual analysis and the impossibility of definitive interpretation *ever* (Fontana 1997: 248, original emphasis).

On the wall in my office at work I have a photo of my four-year-old son gazing at Bosch's painting. What will I say to him when he asks me to interpret the painting? Maybe I can leave the interpretation of the painting hanging, but I cannot leave the interpretation of the rest of his life in a similar relativist ambiguity. He must decide how to act, and I will have to guide him. So while interpretive ambiguity has its pleasures, it cannot remain as an end in itself.

I choose to see the painting as a celebration of pleasure. There are good historical reasons for this interpretation. I am not simply making it up. However, I am fully aware that this choice is as much a personal commitment, reflecting my own values and desires, as it is a choice based on informed reason. I do not pretend it is the only possible interpretation, but I prefer it as an interpretation because of the personal and political implications of that choice.

In the same way, the process of interpreting and analysing qualitative data dances between the worlds of rigorous and reasoned interpretation, imaginative visions, calculated distance and engaged political practice. Analysing and interpreting qualitative data is not only about finding out what the 'other' is thinking and doing, it is also about engaging in an ongoing conversation in which we, as researchers, are unavoidably political participants.

But that is not the final lesson of Bosch's *Garden*. Michel de Certeau (1992) takes us one step further when he argues that it is not adequate to describe *The Garden* as without meaning. Rather, it continually withdraws meaning. The painting contains repeated hints at hidden meaning, and this combined with the multiplicity of possible interpretations leads the viewer to continually search, but never arrive: 'So it is no longer enough to say that this paradise is withdrawn, being-there lying behind the signs that await a good reader. It does not cease *withdrawing*, thanks to the *secrecy effect* it produces, and that active withdrawal is sustained by the decoding activity that the painting entraps by its simulated secrecy' (de Certeau 1992: 51, original emphasis). De Certeau's more general point is that Bosch introduces us to a mystical practice of the withdrawal of meaning that has its contemporary parallel in the postmodernist's perpetual departing.

However, de Certeau is also making a more subtle point about how mysticism as a practice leads to an encounter, if not a dialogue, with the divine other. Perhaps this is more than we can hope for from qualitative research, but I like to think we can see the hints and hear the distant echoes:

> The mystic discourse transforms the detail into myth; it catches hold of it, blows it out of proportion, multiplies it, divinizes it . . . A play of light arrests the reader's attention: ecstatic instant, a spark of insignificance, this fragment of the unknown introduces a silence into the hermeneutic medley. Thus, little by little, common everyday life begins to seethe with a disturbing familiarity—a frequentation of the Other (de Certeau 1992: 10).

Bibliography

Abrahamson, E. and Park, C. 1994 'Concealment of negative organisational outcomes' *Academy of Management Journal*, vol. 37, no. 5, pp. 1302–34.

Alasuutari, P. 1995 *Researching Culture: Qualitative Method and Cultural Studies*, London, Sage.

Altheide, D. 1999 'Fear in the news: a discourse of control' *The Sociological Quarterly*, vol. 40, no. 3, pp. 475–503.

Altheide, D. and Johnson, J. 1994 'Criteria for assessing interpretive validity in qualitative research' in N. Denzin and Y. Lincoln (eds) *Handbook of Qualitative Research*, Thousand Oaks, Sage, pp. 485–99.

Ang, I. 1996 *Living Room Wars*, London, Routledge.

Athens, L. 1984 'Scientific criteria for evaluating qualitative studies' *Studies in Symbolic Interaction*, vol. 5, pp. 259–68.

Atkinson, P. 1990 *The Ethnographic Imagination: Textual Constructions of Reality*, London, Routledge.

Backett-Milburn, K., Mauthner, N. and Parry, O. 1999 'The importance of the conditions of project design for the construction of qualitative data' *International Journal of Social Research Methodology*, vol. 2, no. 4, pp. 297–312.

Bamberg, M. 1997 *Narrative Development: Six Approaches*, London, Lawrence Erlbaum.

Barry, C. 1998 'Choosing qualitative data analysis software: Atlas/ti and Nudist compared' *Sociological Research Online*, vol. 3, no. 3, <http://www.socresonline.org.uk/socresonline/3/3/4.html>

Barthes, R. 1967 *Elements of Semiology*, trans. A. Lavers and C. Smith, London, Jonathan Cape.

——1972 *Mythologies*, New York, Hill & Wang.

Bauman, Z. 1998 'What prospects for morality in times of uncertainty?' *Theory, Culture and Society*, vol. 15, no. 1, pp. 11–22.

——2000 'On writing sociology' *Theory, Culture and Society*, vol. 17, no. 1, pp. 79–90.

167

Becker, H. 1963 *Outsiders*, New York, The Free Press.

——1971 *Sociological Work: Method and Substance*, London, Allen Lane.

——1986 *Writing for Social Scientists*, Chicago, University of Chicago Press.

Becker, H. and Horowitz, I. 1972 'Radical politics and sociological research: observations on methodology and ideology' *American Journal of Sociology*, vol. 78, no. 1, pp. 48–66.

Becker, H. and McCall, M. 1990 *Symbolic Interaction and Cultural Studies*, Chicago, University of Chicago Press.

Bedard, P. 1998 'McCaffrey vows no free needles' *Washington Times*, 29 April p. A1.

Bell, D. 1983 *Daughters of the Dreaming*, Sydney, George Allen & Unwin.

Bell, S. 1999 'Narratives and lives: women's health politics and the diagnosis of cancer for DES daughters' *Narrative Inquiry*, vol. 9, no. 2, pp. 347–89.

Benhabib, S. 1992 *Situating the Self*, London, Routledge.

Bennet, T. 1997 'Towards a pragmatics for cultural studies' in J. McGuigan (ed.) *Cultural Methodologies*, London, Sage.

Bentz, V. and Shapiro, J. 1998 *Mindful Inquiry in Social Research*, London, Sage.

Berger, M. 1986 'Women drivers' *Women's Studies International Forum*, vol. 9, no. 3, pp. 257–63.

Bourdieu, P. [1993] 1999 *The Weight of the World: Social Suffering in Contemporary Society*, Stanford, Stanford University Press.

Brady, I. 2000 'Three jaguar/Mayan intertexts: poetry and prose fiction' *Qualitative Inquiry*, vol. 6, no. 1, pp. 58–65.

Brewer G. 1980 *Out of Work, Out of Sight*, Melbourne, The Brotherhood of St Laurence.

Brown, R. 1991 'Rhetoric, textuality, and the postmodern turn in sociological theory' *Sociological Theory*, vol. 8, no. 2, pp. 188–97.

Bruner, J. 1990 *Acts of Meaning*, Cambridge, MA, Harvard University Press.

Brydon-Miller, M. 1997 'Participatory action research' *Journal of Social Issues*, vol. 53, no. 4, pp. 657–67.

Bryman, A. 2001 *Social Research Methods*, Oxford, Oxford University Press.

Buston, K. 1997 'NUD*IST in action: its use and its usefulness in a study of chronic illness in young people' *Sociological Research Online*, vol. 2, no. 3, <http://www.socresonline.org.uk/socresonline/2/3/6.html>

Calhoun, C. 1994 'Social theory and the politics of identity' in C. Calhoun (ed.) *Social Theory and the Politics of Identity*, Oxford, Blackwell, pp. 9–36.

——1995 *Critical Social Theory*, Oxford, Blackwell.

Carmel, E. 1999 'Concepts, context and discourse in a comparative case study' *International Journal of Social Research Methodology*, vol. 2, no. 2, pp. 141–50.

Carney, J., Joiner, J. and Tragou, H. 1997 'Categorizing, coding, and manipulating qualitative data using the WordPerfect®+ word processor' *The Qualitative Report*, vol. 3, no. 1, <http://www.nova.edu/ssss/QR/QR3-1/carney.html>

Charmaz, K. 1983 'The grounded theory method' in R. Emerson (ed.) *Contemporary Field Research: A Collection of Writings*, Prospect Heights, Waveland Press,

——1995 'Grounded theory' in J. Smith, R. Harre and L. Van Langenhove (eds) *Rethinking Methods in Psychology*, London, Sage, pp. 27–49.

Chase, S. 1995 *Ambiguous Empowerment*, Amherst, University of Massachusetts Press.

——1996 'Personal vulnerability and interpretive authority in narrative research' in R. Josselson (ed.) *Ethics and Process in the Narrative Study of Lives*, vol. 4, London, Sage, pp. 45–59.

Cheatwood, D. 1997 'Making sense and making a difference: murder and college administration' *Qualitative Sociology*, vol. 20, no. 4, pp. 533–41.

Chodorow, N. 1978 *The Reproduction of Mothering: Psychoanalysis and the Sociology of Gender*, Berkeley, University of California Press.

Church, K. 1995 *Forbidden Narratives: Critical Autobiography as Social Science*, Luxembourg, Gordon & Breach.

——1997 *Because of Where We've Been: The Business Behind the Business of Psychiatric Survivor Economic Development*, Ontario, Ontario Council of Alternative Business.

Church, K. and Creal, L. 1995 *Voices of Experience: Five Tales of Community Economic Development in Toronto*, Toronto, Community Economic Development.

Clough, P. 1992 *The End(s) of Ethnography*, Newbury Park, Sage.

Coates, J., Dodds, M. and Jensen, J. 1998 '"Isn't just being here political enough?" Feminist action-oriented research as a challenge to graduate women's studies' *Feminist Studies*, vol. 24, no. 2, pp. 333–47.

Coffey, A., Holbrook, B. and Atkinson, P. 1996 'Qualitative data analysis: technologies and representations' *Sociological Research Online*, vol. 1, no. 1, <http://www.socresonline.org.uk/1/1/4.html>

Collins, P. 1990 *Black Feminist Thought*, New York, Routledge.

——1997 'Comment on Hekman's "Truth and Method"' *Signs*, vol. 22, no. 2, pp. 375–82.

Corbin, J. and Strauss, A. 1990 'Grounded theory research: procedures, canons, and evaluative criteria' *Qualitative Sociology*, vol. 13, no. 1, pp. 3–21.

Cotterill, P. and Letherby, G. 1993 'Weaving stories: personal auto/biographies in feminist research' *Sociology*, vol. 27, no. 1, pp. 67–80.

Cress, D. and Snow, D. 1996 'Mobilization at the margins' *American Sociological Review*, vol. 61, no. 6, pp. 1089–109.

Crisp, R. 2000 'A qualitative study of the perceptions of individuals with disabilities concerning health and rehabilitation professionals' *Disability and Society*, vol. 15, no. 2, pp. 355–67.

Crotty, M. 1998 *The Foundations of Social Research*, Sydney, Allen & Unwin.

Daly, J. 1997 'Reading around review' unpublished paper, La Trobe University, Melbourne.

Daly, J., Kellehear, A. and Gliksman, M. 1997 *The Public Health Researcher*, Melbourne, Oxford University Press.

Daly, K. 1997 'Re-placing theory ethnography: a postmodern view' *Qualitative Inquiry*, vol. 3, no. 3, pp. 343–66.

Davidman, L. 1999 'The personal, the sociological, and the intersection of the two' in B. Glassner and R. Hertz (eds) *Qualitative Sociology as Everyday Life*, Thousand Oaks, Sage, pp. 79–87.

Davies, M. 1997 'Shattered assumptions: time and the experience of long-term HIV positivity' *Social Science and Medicine*, vol. 44, no. 4, pp. 561–71.

Davis, W. 1972 *Peirce's Epistemology*, The Hague, Martinus Nijhoff.

de Certeau, M. 1992 *The Mystic Fable*, trans. M. Smith, Chicago, University of Chicago Press.

De Vault, M. 1996 'Talking back to sociology: distinctive contributions to feminist methodology' *Annual Review of Sociology*, vol. 22, pp. 29–51.

Denzin, N. 1989 *Interpretive Interactionism*, Newbury Park, Sage.

——1992 *Symbolic Interactionism and Cultural Studies*, Oxford, Blackwell.

——1996a 'Prophetic pragmatism and the postmodern: a comment on Maines' *Symbolic Interaction*, vol. 19, no. 4, pp. 341–55.

——1996b 'Punishing poets' *Qualitative Sociology*, vol. 19, no. 4, pp. 525–8.

——1997 *Interpretive Ethnography*, Newbury Park, Sage.

Derrida, J. 1976 *Of Grammatology*, trans. G. Spivak, Baltimore, John Hopkins University Press.

Devault, M. 1999 'Are we alone?' in B. Glassner and R. Hertz (eds) *Qualitative Sociology as Everyday Life*, Thousand Oaks, Sage, pp. 89–96.

Dickson, G. 2000 '"Aboriginal grandmothers" experience with health promotion and participatory action research' *Qualitative Health Research*, vol. 10, no. 2, pp. 188–213.

Dohan, D. and Sancheq-Jankowski, M. 1998 'Using computers to analyze ethnographic field data' *Annual Review of Sociology*, vol. 24, no. 1, pp. 477–99.

Eco, U. 1983 'Horns, hooves, insteps: some hypotheses on three types of abduction' in U. Eco and T. Sebeok (eds) *The Sign of Three*, Bloomington, IN, Indiana University Press.

Ellis, C. 1995a 'Speaking of dying: an ethnographic short story' *Symbolic Interaction*, vol. 18, no. 1, pp. 73–81.

——1995b *Final Negotiations*, Philadelphia, Temple University Press.

Elshtain, J. 1981 *Public Man, Private Woman*, Oxford, Martin Robertson.

Emerson, R. 1983 *Contemporary Field Research*, Boston, Little Brown & Co.

Erickson, K. 1976 *Everything in its Path: Destruction of the Community in the Buffalo Creek Flood*, New York, Simon & Schuster.

Estroff, S. 1995 'Whose story is it anyway?' in S. Toombs, D. Barnard and R. Carson (eds) *Chronic Illness: From Experience to Policy*, Bloomington, IN, Indiana University Press, pp. 77–102.

Evans, L. and Davies, K. 2000 'No sissy boys here: A content analysis of the representation of masculinity in elementary school reading text-books' *Sex Roles*, vol. 42, nos 3/4, pp. 255–70.

Eyler, A., Baker, E., Cromer, L., King, A., Brownson, R. and Donatello, R. 1998 'Physical activity and minority women' *Health Education and Behavior*, vol. 25, no. 5, pp. 560–652.

Ezzy, D. 1993 'Unemployment and mental health' *Social Science and Medicine*, vol. 37, no. 1, pp. 41–52.

——1997 'Subjectivity and the labour process: conceptualising "good work" ' *Sociology*, vol. 31, no. 3, pp. 427–44.

——2000a 'Illness narratives: time, hope and HIV' *Social Science and Medicine*, vol. 50, no. 5, pp. 605–17.

——2000b 'Fate and agency in job loss narratives' *Qualitative Sociology*, vol. 23, no. 1, pp. 121–34.

——2000c 'Reading for the plot, and not hearing the story: ecological tragedy and heroic capitalism' in A. Mills and J. Smith (eds) *Utter Silence: Voicing the Unspeakable in Contemporary Culture*, New York, Peter Lang, pp. 67–82.

Ezzy, D., de Visser, R., Bartos, M., McDonald, K., O'Donnell, D. and Rosenthal D. 1998 *HIV Futures Community Report*, Melbourne, National Centre in HIV Social Research, La Trobe University.

Ezzy, D., Grubb, I., de Visser, R. and McConachy, D. 1997 *People Living with HIV/AIDS Snapshots: Treatments, Accommodation and Employment*, Melbourne, National Centre in HIV Social Research, La Trobe University.

Farberman, H. 1992 'The grounds of critique' *Symbolic Interaction*, vol. 15, pp. 375–9.

Fee, D. 1992 'Symbolic interaction and postmodern possibilities' *Symbolic Interaction*, vol. 15, pp. 367–73.

Fielding, N. and Lee, R. 1998 *Computer Analysis and Qualitative Research*, London, Sage.

Fine, G. 1998 *Morel Tales: The Culture of Mushrooming*, Cambridge, MA, Harvard University Press.

Fine, M. 1994 'Working the hyphens: reinventing self and other in qualitative research' in N. Denzin and Y. Lincoln (eds) *Handbook of Qualitative Research*, Thousand Oaks, Sage, pp. 70–82.

Fiske, J. and Hartley, J. 1978 *Reading Television*, London, Routledge.

Fontana, A. 1997 'Of heaven and hell: narrating Hieronymus Bosch' *Qualitative Inquiry*, vol. 3, no. 2, pp. 237–49.

Foucault, M. 1977 *Discipline and Punish*, Harmondsworth, Penguin.

——1980 *Power/Knowledge*, New York, Pantheon Books.

Frank, A. 1995 *The Wounded Storyteller*, Chicago, University of Chicago Press.

Franzosi, R. 1998 'Narrative analysis' *Annual Review of Sociology*, vol. 24, no. 1, pp. 517–55.

Freeman, M. 1984 'History, narrative, and life-span developmental knowledge' *Human Development*, vol. 27, no. 1, pp. 1–19.

Gadamer, H. 1975 *Truth and Method*, trans. J. Weinsheimer and D. Marshall, London, Sheed & Ward.

Game, A. 1991 *Undoing the Social: Toward a Deconstructive Sociology*, Milton Keynes, Open University Press.

Garratt, D. and Hodkinson, P. 1998 'Can there be criteria for selecting research criteria? A hermeneutical analysis of an inescapable dilemma' *Qualitative Inquiry*, vol. 4, no. 4, pp. 515–30.

Garrett, C. 1998 *Beyond Anorexia: Narrative, Spirituality and Recovery*, Cambridge, Cambridge University Press.

Geertz, C. 1973 *The Interpretation of Cultures*, New York, Basic Books.

Gergen, M. 1988 'Narrative structures in social explanation' in C. Antaki (ed.) *Analysing Everyday Explanation*, London, Sage, pp. 94–112.

——1992 'Life stories: pieces of a dream' in G. Rosenwald and R. Ochberg (eds) *Storied Lives: The Cultural Politics of Self-Understanding*, New Haven & London, Yale University Press, pp. 127–44.

Gersen, E. 1991 'Supplementing grounded theory' in D. Maines (ed.) *Social Organisation and Social Process*, New York, Aldine De Gruytes, pp. 285–302.

Glaser, B. 1978 *Theoretical Sensitivity*, Mill Valley, Sociology Press.

Glaser, B. and Strauss, A. 1965a 'Temporal aspects of dying as a non-scheduled status passage' *American Journal of Sociology*, vol. 71, pp. 48–58.

——1965b *Awareness of Dying*, London, Weidenfeld & Nicolson.

——1967 *The Discovery of Grounded Theory*, Chicago, Aldine.

Glassner, B. and Hertz, R. (eds) 1999 *Qualitative Sociology as Everyday Life*, Thousand Oaks, Sage.

Goffman, E., 1961 *Asylums*, Harmondsworth, Penguin.

——1989 'On fieldwork' *Journal of Contemporary Ethnography*, vol. 18, no. 2, pp. 123–32.

Gouldner, A. 1975 *For Sociology*, Harmondsworth, Penguin.

Green, J. 1998 'Commentary: grounded theory and the constant comparative method' *British Medical Journal*, vol. 316, no. 7137, pp. 1064–5.

Grey, C. 1994 'Career as a project of the self and labour process discipline' *Sociology*, vol. 28, no. 2, pp. 479–97.

Grossberg, L. 1998 '"The cultural studies" crossroads blues' *European Journal of Cultural Studies*, vol. 1, no. 1, pp. 65–82.

Guba, E. 1984 'The effect of definitions of policy on the nature and outcomes of policy analysis' *Educational Leadership*, vol. 42 pp. 1–33.

Gubrium, J. and Holstein, J. 1997 *The New Language of Qualitative Method*, New York, Oxford University Press.

Hall, B. 1981 'Participatory research, popular knowledge, and power' *Convergence*, vol. 14, no. 1, pp. 6–17.

Hall, S. 1980 'Encoding/decoding' in S. Hall, D. Hobson, A. Lows, P. Willis (eds) *Culture, Media, Language*, London, Hutchinson.

Hamer, J. 1997 'The fathers of "fatherless" black children' *Families in Society*, vol. 78, no. 6, pp. 564–78.

Hammersley, M. 1998 *Reading Ethnographic Research*, 2nd edn, London, Longman.

Haraway, D. 1988 'Situated knowledges: the science question in feminism and the privilege of partial perspective' *Feminist Studies*, vol. 14, no. 3, pp. 575–99.

Harding, S. 1986 *The Science Question in Feminism*, New York, Cornell University Press.

——1987 *Feminism and Methodology*, Milton Keynes, Open University Press.

——1997 'Comment on Hekman's "Truth and Method"' *Signs*, vol. 22, no. 2, pp. 382–92.

Harris, J. and Goldstein, A. 1998 'Puncturing an AIDS initiative' *Washington Post*, 23 April, p. A1.

Harstock, N. 1983 *Money, Sex, and Power*, New York, Longman.

Heaton, J. 1998 'Secondary analysis of qualitative data' *Social Research Update*, no. 22, <http://www.soc.surrey.ac.uk/sru/SRU22.html>

Hebdige, D. 1979 *Subculture*, London, Routledge.

Heckert, D. and Best, A. 1997 'Ugly duckling to swan: labelling theory and the stigmatization of red hair' *Symbolic Interaction*, vol. 20, no. 4, pp. 365–84.

Heelan, P. and Schulkin, J. 1998 'Hermeneutical philosophy and pragmatism: a philosophy of science' *Synthese*, vol. 115, no. 3, pp. 269–302.

Heidegger, M. 1962 *Being and Time*, trans. J. Macquarie and E. Robinson, Oxford, Blackwell.

Hekman, S. 1997 'Truth and method: feminist standpoint theory revisited' *Signs*, vol. 22, no. 2, pp. 341–66.

Herndl, C, and Nahrwold, C. 2000 'Research as social practice' *Written Communication*, vol. 17, no. 2, pp. 258–96.

Hertz, R. 1996 'Introduction: ethics, reflexivity and voice' *Qualitative Sociology*, vol. 19, no. 1, pp. 3–9.

Hintz, R. and Miller, D. 1995 'Openings revisited: the foundations of social interaction' *Symbolic Interaction*, vol. 18, no. 3, pp. 355–69.

Hirsch, M., Conforti, R. and Graney, C. 1990 'The use of marijuana for pleasure' *Journal of Social Behavior and Personality*, vol. 5, no. 4, pp. 497–510.

Holloway, W. and Jefferson, T. 1997 'Eliciting narrative through the in-depth interview' *Qualitative Inquiry*, vol. 3, no. 1, pp. 53–71.

Holstein, J. and Gubrium, J. 1995 *The Active Interview*, Thousand Oaks, Sage.

Huber, J. 1995 'Centennial essay: institutional perspectives on sociology' *American Journal of Sociology*, vol. 101, no. 1, pp. 194–216.

Hume, L. 1997 *Witchcraft and Paganism in Australia*, Melbourne, Melbourne University Press.

——1999 'Witches of the Southern Cross: the sacred places and sacred space of modern Australian witches' *Journal of Australian Studies*, vol. 12, no. 1, pp. 95–107.

Irvine, L. 1999 *Codependent Forevermore: The Invention of Self in a Twelve Step Group*, Chicago, University of Chicago Press.

Jagger E. 1998 'Marketing the self, buying the other' *Sociology*, vol. 32, no. 4, pp. 195–212.

Jayaratne, T. and Stewart, A. 1991 'Quantitative and qualitative methods in the social sciences: current feminist issues and practical strategies' in M. Fonow and J. Cook, *Beyond Methodology: Feminist Scholarship as Lived Research*, Bloomington, IN, Indiana University Press.

Johnson, M. 1999 'Observations on positivism and pseudoscience in qualitative nursing research' *Journal of Advanced Nursing*, vol. 30, no. 1, pp. 67–73.

Jones, M. 1983 *The Australian Welfare State*, Sydney, George Allen & Unwin.

Josselson, R. 1995 'Narrative interpretations' in R. Josselson and A. Lieblich (eds) *Interpreting Experience: The Narrative Study of Lives*, vol. 3, Thousand Oaks, Sage, pp. 29–45.

Josselson, R. and Leiblich, E. (eds) 1993 *The Narrative Study of Lives*, vol. 1, London, Sage.

Joy, M. 1993 'Feminism and the self' *Theory and Psychology*, vol. 3, no. 3, pp. 275–302.

Karp, D., 1996 *Speaking of Sadness, Depression, Disconnection and the Meanings of Illness*, New York, Oxford University Press.

Karp, D., Holmstrom, L. and Gray, P. 1998 'Leaving home for college' *Symbolic Interaction*, vol. 21, no. 3, pp. 253–76.

Katovich, M. and Reese, W. 1993 'Postmodern thought in symbolic interaction: reconstructing social inquiry in light of late-modern concerns' *Sociological Quarterly*, vol. 34, no. 3, pp. 391–411.

Kearny, R. 1999 *Poetics of Modernity: Toward a Hermeneutic Imagination*, New York, Humanity Books.

Kelle, U. 1997 'Theory building in qualitative research and computer programs for the management of textual data'*Sociological Research Online*, vol. 2, no. 2, <http://www.socresonline.org.uk/socresonline/2/2/1.html>

Kellehear, A. 1993 *The Unobtrusive Researcher*, Sydney, Allen & Unwin.

Kendall, J. 1999 'Axial coding and the grounded theory controversy' *Western Journal of Nursing Research*, vol. 21, no. 6, pp. 743–57.

Kvale, S. 1995 'The social construction of validity' *Qualitative Inquiry*, vol. 1, no. 1, pp. 19–40.

Lalli, P. 1989 'The imaginative dimension of everyday life: towards a hermeneutic reading' *Current Sociology*, vol. 37, no. 1, pp. 103–14.

Lamont, M. and Wuthnow, R. 1990 'Betwixt and between: recent cultural sociology in Europe and the United States' in G. Ritzer (ed.) *Frontiers of Social Theory*, New York, Columbia University Press.

Landauer, T. 1996 *The Trouble with Computers*, Bradford, MIT Press.

Lather, P. 1991 *Getting Smart: Feminist Research and Pedagogy With/in the Postmodern*, New York, Routledge.

——1993 'Fertile obsession: validity after poststructuralism' *The Sociological Quarterly*, vol. 34, no. 4, pp. 673–93.

——1997 'Drawing the line at angels: working the ruins of feminist ethnography' *Qualitative Studies in Education*, vol. 10, no. 3, pp. 285–304.

Lather, P. and Smithies, C. 1997 *Troubling the Angels: Women Living with HIV/AIDS*, Boulder, HarperCollins.

Lee, R. and Fielding, N. 1991 'Computing for qualitative research' in N. Fielding and R. Lee (eds) (1998) *Using Computers in Qualitative Research*, London, Sage.

——1996 'Qualitative data analysis: representations of a technology: a comment on Coffey, Holbrook and Atkinson' *Sociological Research Online*, vol. 1, no. 4,
<http://www.socresonline.org.uk/socresonline/1/4/lf.html>

Lemert, C. 1994 'Dark thoughts about the self' in C. Calhoun (ed.) *Social Theory and the Politics of Identity*, Oxford, Blackwell.

Lewin, K. 1946 'Action research and minority problems' *Journal of Social Issues*, vol. 2, no. 1, pp. 34–46.

Liberman, K. 1999 'From walkabout to meditation: craft and ethics in field inquiry' *Qualitative Inquiry*, vol. 5, no. 1, pp. 47–63.

Lincoln, Y. 1995 'Emerging criteria for quality in qualitative and interpretive research' *Qualitative Inquiry*, vol. 1, no. 3, pp. 275–89.

Lincoln, Y. and Guba, E. (eds) 1985 *Naturalistic Inquiry*, Thousand Oaks, Sage.

Lindberg, O. 1999 'Grounded theory and computer-assisted analysis of qualitative data', unpublished paper.

Linde, C. 1993 *Life Stories: The Creation of Coherence*, New York, Oxford University Press.

Lofland, J. and Lofland, L. 1971 *Analyzing Social Settings*, 2nd edn, Belmont, CA, Wadsworth.

Long, C. and Curry, M. 1998 'Living in two worlds: native American women and prenatal care' *Health Care for Women International*, vol. 19, no. 2, pp. 205–15.

Long, E. 1997 'Introduction' in E. Long (ed.) *From Sociology to Cultural Studies*, Oxford, Blackwell, pp. 1–9.

Luborsky, M. and Rubinstein, R. 1995 'Sampling in qualitative research' *Research on Aging*, vol. 17, no. 1, pp. 89–113.

Lucy, N. 1995 *Debating Derrida*, Melbourne, Melbourne University Press.

Luhrmann, T. 1989 *Persuasions of the Witch's Craft: Ritual Magic in Contemporary England*, Oxford, Blackwell.

MacIntyre, A. 1995 *After Virtue*, 2nd edn, London, Duckworth.

MacMillan, K. and McLachlan, S. 1999 'Theory-building with NUD*IST: using computer assisted qualitative analysis in a media case study' *Sociological Research Online*, vol. 4, no. 2, <http://www.socresonline. org.uk/socresonline/4/2/macmillan_mcLachlan.html>

Maguire, P. 1987 *Doing Participatory Research:A Feminist Approach*, Amherst, Centre for International Education, University of Massachusetts.

. Maines, D. 1991 (ed.) *Social Organization and Social Process: Essays in Honor of Anselm Strauss*, New York, Aldine de Gruyter.

——1996 'On choices and criticism: a reply to Denzin' *Symbolic Interaction*, vol. 19, no. 4, pp. 357–62.

Mangabeira, W. 1996 'CAQDAS and its diffusion across four countries' *Current Sociology*, vol. 44, no. 3, pp. 191–205.

Manning, K. 1997 'Authenticity in constructivist inquiry' *Qualitative Inquiry*, vol. 3, no. 1, pp. 93–116.

Manning, P. 1992 *Erving Goffman and Modern Sociology*, Stanford, CA, Stanford University Press.

Marshall, H. 1999 'Rigour or rigidity? The role of CAQDAS in qualitative research' paper presented at the Australian Qualitative Research Conference, Melbourne, July 1999.

Martin, W. 1986 *Recent Theories of Narrative*, Ithaca, Cornell University Press.

Mason, J. 1996 *Qualitative Researching*, London, Sage.

Mattingly, C. 1994 'The concept of therapeutic employment' *Social Science and Medicine*, vol. 38, no. 6, pp. 811–22.

Mays, N. and Pope, C. 1995 'Rigour and qualitative research' *British Medical Journal*, vol. 310, no. 6997, pp. 109–13.

McConville, M. 1994 *Standing Accused*, Clarendon, Oxford.

McConville, M., Sanders, A. and Leng, R. 1991 *The Case for the Prosecution*, London: Routledge.

McDonald, K., Bartos, M., de Visser, R., Ezzy, D. and Rosenthal, D. 1998 *Standing on Shifting Sand:Women Living with HIV/AIDS in Australia*, National Centre in HIV Social Research, La Trobe University, Melbourne.

McEachern, C. 1998 'A mutual interest? Ethnography in anthropology and cultural studies' *The Australian Journal of Anthropology*, vol. 9, no. 3, pp. 251–60.

McGettigan, A. 1997 'Uncorrected insight: metaphor and transcendence "after truth" in qualitative inquiry' *Qualitative Inquiry*, vol. 3, no. 3, pp. 366–84.

McGuigan, J. 1992 *Cultural Populism*, London, Routledge.

——1997 'Introduction' in J. McGuigan (ed.) *Cultural Methodologies*, London, Sage, pp. 1–11.

McKinley, E. 1997 *Beverly Hills 90210*, Pennsylvania, University of Pennsylvania Press.

McLennan, G. 1995 'Feminism, epistemology and postmodernism' *Sociology*, vol. 29, no. 3, pp. 391–410.

McLeod, M. and Nott, P. 1994 *A Place to Belong*, Sydney, Australian Federation of AIDS Organisations.

Melrose, R. 1995 'The seduction of abduction: Peirce's theory of signs and indeterminacy in language' *Journal of Pragmatics*, vol. 23, no. 5, pp. 493–507.

Merleau-Ponty, M. 1962 *Phenomenology of Perception*, trans. C. Smith, London, Routledge.

Mies, M. 1991 'Women's research or feminist research?' in M. Fonow and J. Cook (eds) *Beyond Methodology: Feminist Scholarship as Lived Research*, Bloomington, IN, Indiana University Press, pp. 60–84.

Miles, M. and Huberman, A. 1994 *Qualitative Data Analysis: A Sourcebook of New Methods*, 2nd edn, Thousand Oaks, Sage.

Miller, D., Creswell, J. and Olander, L. 1998 'Writing and retelling multiple ethnographic tales of a soup kitchen for the homeless' *Qualitative Inquiry*, vol. 4, no. 4, pp. 469–80.

Mills, C. 1959 *The Sociological Imagination*, Harmondsworth, Penguin.

Minichiello, V., Aroni, R., Timewell, E. and Alexander, L. 1990 *In-depth Interviewing: Researching People*, Melbourne, Longman Cheshire.

Mishler, E. 1986 *Research Interviewing: Context and Narrative*, Cambridge, MA, Harvard University Press.

——1990 'Validation in inquiry-guided research: the role of exemplars in narrative studies' *Harvard Educational Review*, vol. 60, no. 3, pp. 415–42.

Morris, M. 1990 'Banality in cultural studies' in P. Mellencamp (ed.) *Logics of Television*, Bloomington, IN, Indiana University Press.

Morrow, S. and Smith, M. 1995 'Constructions of survival and coping by women who have survived childhood sexual abuse' *Journal of Counselling Psychology*, vol. 42, no. 1, pp. 24–34.

Moustakas, C. 1994 *Phenomenological Research Methods*, Thousand Oaks, Sage.

Mykhalovskiy, E. 1996 'Reconsidering table talk: critical thoughts on the relationship between sociology, autobiography and self-indulgence' *Qualitative Sociology*, vol. 19, no. 1, pp. 131–51.

Nelson, G., Ochocka, J., Griffin, K. and Lord, J. 1998 '"Nothing about me, without me": participatory action research with self-help/mutual aid organizations for psychiatric consume/survivors' *American Journal of Community Psychology*, vol. 26, no. 6, pp. 881–912.

New, C. 1998 'Realism, deconstruction and the feminist standpoint' *Journal for the Theory of Social Behaviour*, vol. 28, no. 4, pp. 349–72.

Nightingale, V. 1993 'What's "ethnographic" about ethnographic audience research?' in J. Frow and M. Morris (eds) *Australian Cultural Studies*, Urbana, University of Illinois Press, pp. 149–61.

Oakley, A. 1998 'Gender, methodology and people's ways of knowing' *Sociology*, vol. 34, no. 4, pp. 707–31.

Olesen, V. 1994 'Feminisms and models of qualitative research' in N. Denzin and Y. Lincoln (eds) *Handbook of Qualitative Research*, Thousand Oaks, Sage, pp. 158–74.

Orona, C. 1990 'Temporality and identity loss due to Alzheimer's disease' *Social Science and Medicine*, vol. 30, no. 11, pp. 1247–56.

Parsons, T. and Bales, F. 1955 *Family, Socialization, and Interaction Process*, Glencoe, IL, Free Press.

Patton, M. 1990 *Qualitative Evaluation and Research Methods*, 2nd edn, Newbury Park, Sage.

Peirce, C.S. 1965 *Collected Papers*, C. Hartshorne and P. Weiss (eds), Cambridge, MA, Harvard University Press.

Personal Narratives Group 1989 *Interpreting Women's Lives*, Bloomington, IN, Indiana University Press.

Polkinghorne, D. 1988 *Narrative Knowing and the Human Sciences*, Albany, State University of New York Press.

Potter, J. 1996 *Representing Reality: Discourse, Rhetoric and Social Construction*, London, Sage.

Prus, R. 1996 *Symbolic Interaction and Ethnographic Research*, Albany, State University of New York Press.

Qualitative Solutions Research 1999 'The new qualitative coding' *QSR Insight*, vol. 2, no. 1, p. 1.

Radaway, J. 1991 *Reading the Romance: Women, Patriarchy, and Popular Literature*, Chapel Hill, University of North Carolina Press.

Reason, P. 1993 'Reflections on sacred experience and sacred science' *Journal of Management Inquiry*, vol. 2, no. 3, pp. 273–83.

Reinharz, S. 1992 *Feminist Methods in Social Research*, New York, Oxford University Press.

Rice, P. and Ezzy, D. 1999 *Qualitative Research Methods: A Health Focus*, Melbourne, Oxford University Press.

Richards, L. 1999 'Computer monitor: data alive!' *Qualitative Health Research*, vol. 9, no. 3, pp. 412–28.

Richardson, L. 1991 'Postmodern social theory' *Sociological Theory*, vol. 9, no. 1, pp. 173–9.

——1994 'Writing: a method of inquiry' in N. Denzin and Y. Lincoln (eds) *Handbook of Qualitative Research*, Thousand Oaks, Sage, pp. 516–29.

——1996 'A sociology of responsibility' *Qualitative Sociology*, vol. 19, no. 4, pp. 519–24.

——1997 *Fields of Play: Constructing an Academic Life*, New Brunswick, Rutgers University Press.

Richter, K. 1993 'Computerizing ethnographic data' in B. Yoddumnern-Attig, G. Attig, W. Boonchalaski, K. Richter and A. Soonthorndhada (eds) *Qualitative Methods for Population and Health Research*, Institute for Population and Social Research, Mahidol University, Salaya, Thailand.

Ricoeur, P. 1984 *Time and Narrative*, vol. 1, Chicago, University of Chicago Press.

——1985 *Time and Narrative*, vol. 2, Chicago, University of Chicago Press.

——1988 *Time and Narrative*, vol. 3, Chicago, University of Chicago Press.

——1992 *Oneself as Another*, trans. Kathleen Blamey, Chicago, University of Chicago Press.

Riessman, C. 1993 *Narrative Analysis*, Newbury Park, Sage.

Ring, A. 1997 'Keeping the sexist flame alive: why do magazines keep doing it?' *Australian Studies in Journalism*, vol. 6, no. 1, pp. 3–40.

Risser, J. 1997 *Hermeneutics and the Voice of the Other*, Albany, State University of New York Press.

Rist, R. 1994 'Influencing the policy process with qualitative research' in N. Denzin and Y. Lincoln (eds) *Handbook of Qualitative Research*, Thousand Oaks, Sage, pp. 545–58.

Ronai, C. 1998 'Sketching with Derrida: an ethnography of a researcher/erotic dancer' *Qualitative Inquiry*, vol. 4, no. 4, pp. 405–21.

Rorty, R. 1996 'Solidarity or objectivity?' in R. Rorty (ed.) *Objectivity, Relativism and Truth*, Cambridge, MA, Cambridge University Press.

Rosaldo, R. 1989 *Culture and Truth*, London, Routledge.

Rubin, H. and Rubin, I. 1995 *Qualitative Interviewing: The Art of Hearing Data*, Thousand Oaks, Sage.

Ryan, G. 1993 'Using WordPerfect® macros to handle fieldnotes' *Cultural Anthropology Methods*, vol. 5, no. 1, pp. 10–11.

Sansom, C. 1959 *The World of Poetry*, London, Phoenix House.

Schatzman, L. 1991 'Dimensional analysis' in D. Maines (ed.) *Social Organization and Social Process*, New York, Aldine de Gruyter, pp. 303–14.

Schwalbe, M. 1995 'The responsibilities of sociological poets' *Qualitative Sociology*, vol. 18, no. 4, pp. 393–413.

Sebeok T. 1983 'One, two, three spells UBERTY' in U. Eco and T. Sebeok (eds), *The Sign of Three*, Bloomington, IN, Indiana University Press.

Seidel J. 1998 'Qualitative data Analysis' <http://www.qualisresearch.com>

Shank, G. 2001 'It's logic in practice, my dear Watson: an imaginary memoir from beyond the grave' *Forum Qualitative Sozialforschung/ Forum: Qualitative Social Research* [On-line journal], 2 (1), 2001. Available at <http://qualitative-research.net/fqs/fqs-eng.htm>

Shiner, M. and Newburn, T. 1997 'Definitely, maybe not? The normalisation of recreational drug use amongst young people' *Sociology*, vol. 31, pp. 511–29.

Smith, D. 1974 'Women's perspective as a radical critique of sociology' *Sociological Inquiry*, vol. 44, no. 1, pp. 7–14.

——1987 *The Everyday World as Problematic: A Feminist Sociology*, Milton Keynes, Open University Press.

——1997 'Comment on Hekman's "truth and method"' *Signs*, vol. 22, no. 2, pp. 392–99.

Smith, P. 1998 'The new American cultural sociology' in P. Smith, (ed.) *The New American Cultural Sociology*, Cambridge, Cambridge University Press, pp. 1–14.

Snow, D. and Anderson, L. 1993 *Down on Their Luck: A Study of Homeless Street People*, Berkeley, University of California Press.

Somers, M. and Gibson, G. 1994 'Reclaiming the epistemological "other"' in C. Calhoun (ed.) *Social Theory and the Politics of Identity*, Oxford, Blackwell.

Spall, S. 1998 'Peer debriefing in qualitative research' *Qualitative Inquiry*, vol. 4, no. 2, pp. 280–93.

Spence, D. 1988 'Tough and tender-minded hermeneutics' in S. Messer, L. Saas, R. Woolfolk (eds) *Hermeneutics and Phychological Theory*, New Brunswick and London, Rutgers University Press, pp. 62–84.

Stanley, L. 1990 'Feminism and the academic mode' in L. Stanley (ed.) *Feminist Praxis*, London, Routledge.

——1993 'On auto/biography in sociology' *Sociology*, vol. 27, no. 1, pp. 41–53.

Stevens, P. and Doerr, B. 1997 'Trauma of discovery: women's narratives of being informed they are HIV-infected' *AIDS Care*, vol. 9, no. 5, pp. 523–38.

Strauss, A. 1987 *Qualitative Analysis for Social Scientists*, Cambridge, Cambridge University Press.

Strauss, A. and Corbin, J. 1990 *Basics of Qualitative Research*, London, Sage.

Tate, J. 1998 'The hermeneutic circle vs. the enlightenment' *Telos*, no. 110, pp. 9–38.

Taylor, C. 1989 *Sources of the Self*, Cambridge, Cambridge University Press.

——1992 *Ethics of Authenticity*, Cambridge, MA, Harvard University Press.

Textsmart 2000 <http://www.spss.com/textsmart/example.htm> June 2000

Thomas, W. 1928 *The Child in America*, New York, Knopf.

Thorne, B. 1980 ' "You still takin' notes?" Fieldwork and the problems of informed consent' *Social Problems*, vol. 27, no. 2, pp. 284–97.

Torre, C. 1995 'Chaos, creativity and innovation' in R. Robertson and A. Combs (eds) *Chaos Theory in Psychology and the Life Sciences*, Mahwah, NJ, Lawrence Erlbaum.

Travers, M. 1997 'Preaching to the converted? Improving the persuasiveness of criminal justice research' *British Journal of Criminology*, vol. 37, no. 2, pp. 359–77.

Trigger, B. 1989 'Hyperrelativism, responsibility, and the social sciences' *Canadian Review of Sociology and Anthropology*, vol. 26, no. 5, pp. 776–97.

Turnbull, W. 1986 'Everyday explanation: the pragmatics of puzzle resolution' *Journal for the Theory of Social Behaviour*, vol. 16, pp. 141–60.

Van Maanen, J. 1988 *Tales of the Field: On Writing Ethnography*, Chicago, The University of Chicago Press.

Wacquant, L. 1998 'Pierre Bourdieu' in R. Stones (ed.) *Key Sociological Thinkers*, London, Macmillan.

Way, N. 1997 'Using feminist research methods to understand the friendships of adolescent boys' *Journal of Social Issues*, vol. 53, no. 4, pp. 703–24.

Weil, S. 1989 'On human personality' in D. McLellan, *Simone Weil, Utopian Pessimist*, London, Macmillan, pp. 273–88.

Weiss, C. 1982 'Evaluations for decisions' *Evaluation Practice*, vol. 9, no. 1, pp. 101–22.

Weitzman, E. and Miles, M. 1995 *Computer Programs for Qualitative Data Analysis*, Thousand Oaks, Sage.

Willis, P. 1977 *Learning to Labour*, Farnborough, Saxon House.

Windschuttle, K. 1979 *Unemployment*, Melbourne, Penguin.

Wuest, J. 2000 'Negotiating with helping systems: an example of grounded theory evolving through emergent fit' *Qualitative Health Research*, vol. 10, no. 1, pp. 51–70.

Yeich, S. 1996 'Grassroots organizing with homeless people: a participatory research approach' *Journal of Social Issues*, vol. 52, no. 1, pp. 111–22.

Index